Keeping My
Sister

Keeping My Sister
A story of sibling survivalry
By Nancy Paul

Nancy Paul
Indianapolis
317-755-0434
desprithousewife.com
nancyschmollpaul@gmail.com

ISBN: 9780989438834

Library of Congress Control Number: 2014901039

Cover and interior design: Suzanne Parada
Editor: Janet Schwind
Photography: Steve Polston
Author Photography: Ian Smith

Keeping My
Sister

A story of sibling survivalry

NANCY PAUL

"When the little girl speaks, healing will come."
—Becky Winnie

Dedicated to Mandy and Kristine and Kim,
who helped me remember her voice,

To Mom and Dad who encouraged me to share it,

And to our Heavenly Father who emboldens
me to use mine.

Special thank you to Janet Schwind,
my supernaturally gifted editor and friend.
I heard her again for the first time in
twenty years because of you.

CONTENTS

PROLOGUE

When I woke up, I wasn't in my own bed. The glow of the fire in the gas furnace flickered in the darkness of the old farmhouse. By its light I made out various lumps of men and women passed out all over the living room floor. They snored...twitched...rolled over to find more comfortable positions on the filthy matted carpet, but did not wake.

My younger sister lay on the floor, too. The reflection of the flames danced over her hair. Long and blonde, it cascaded over her pillow and covered most of her face. She was asleep on her stomach, arms down at her sides, mouth slack, drool plastering her hair to her cheek. She snored gently.

She was wearing her favorite soft, yellow blanket jammies; I wore my orange pair. She and I often raced to see who could skate the farthest across the sticky linoleum in our white footies. Both outfits were well worn and pulled tight against our growing seven- and five-year-old legs. Mom had mentioned cutting off the feet so we could wear them longer, which sent us both into hysterics. How would we slide across the kitchen floor?

I stretched out my legs. My foot bumped against something hard. An ashtray overturned. I sat up, pushed the ashes into the carpet, righted the glass bowl and replaced as many cigarette butts as I could feel in the darkness. I moved away from the mess, pushed an empty vodka bottle away from my pillow and lay back down. There were beer cans, lighters and cigarette boxes all over the floor. Overflowing ashtrays along with a few pipes and roach clips sat on the coffee table. A tall homemade bong was its centerpiece.

There were few blankets covering the sleepers. The one I had was a red, yellow and black plaid. I wrapped it tightly around my body. I closed my eyes, but only for a moment, because I felt his eyes boring into the back of my neck. I turned over and looked toward the chair on the other side of the room. He was sitting there, smiling at me in the darkness, teeth gleaming white.

Alarmed, I recognized him immediately. He had visited me in my bedroom before. He had been quiet and gentle. I didn't understand the things he had done or said to me, but he had not caused me pain. Yet I feared and wanted to avoid him, so I shrunk back into myself and scrunched my eyes tight, hoping in a childish belief that if I couldn't see him he couldn't see me either.

The furnace shut down then, leaving the room in total blackness. I panicked and blindly threw off the blanket and ran to my bedroom. I wanted to dive under the heavy quilt and hide, but stopped short and blankly stared at the couple who were sleeping soundly in my bed. I thought about asking them to leave, but realized there was no use; my bed hadn't been safe from him in the past anyway.

I didn't know what to do next. If I were able to wake an adult, what would I say? That there was a man awake in the living room? I was pretty sure I would just get a slurred, "Go back to sleep." I knew leaving the house wasn't an option. I'd tried running away once when I was younger, but ended up sitting under a tree in the front yard because I knew better than to cross the road myself. Also, I was scared of the landlord's vicious dogs, who roamed around the fields at night.

I thought of the closet and remembered it had always been a place to use our imaginations. My sister and I sometimes stripped down to our shorts in my locker room closet and pretended to be the boxers we'd watched on TV, jabbing and ducking on my boxing ring bed. One time I left her there to get a shirt for myself from the laundry basket on the living room couch. When I got back to my room, I simultaneously smelled smoke and heard fists pounding on our front door. "Fire! Fire!" hollered our neighbor boys as they stormed in to take us out to the yard. My sister threw such a huge fit about not having a shirt on that one of the boys had to run back in to get one for her.

On this night, instead of pretending it was a locker room, I needed to pretend it was a safe vault. I entered quietly, imagining the large impenetrable steel door click heavily shut behind me, combination lock engaged. I made a nest of the dirty clothes lying on the floor and lay my head on a teddy bear. A hole made by a cigarette burn scratched at my ear. Flipping it over, I curled up with my knees pulled up to my chest and for the first time in a long time, stuck my thumb in my mouth.

I began to drift off to sleep, absently thinking about what I would do the next day. The farm we rented provided endless opportunities for adventure. We could climb up into the fort we'd found in the rafters of an old outbuilding, ride our bikes to the neighbor's dairy farm and play "bikers," or if were brave enough, walk across the cow-patty-covered fields to the cave we'd discovered and venture in. We had kittens to play with, gooseberries to pick, haymows to jump in and trees to climb.

We had faced many dangers together, too. There was the barbed wire fence at the bottom of the sledding hill, which would have beheaded me had my sister not yelled, "Duck!" at the last minute. There was the old school desk she'd played on like a teeter totter. "Stop!" I yelled when I saw the danger. Wide-eyed, she had leaned towards me, but that didn't keep her from falling backward out of the window. Huge, jagged pieces of glass stuck into the soft skin of her back. Had she landed a few inches over it would have been on the door to the storm cellar and glass would have pushed through into her internal organs.

Alone in my closet, half asleep, my thoughts snapped back to the current danger, the one I was facing without her. My sister was my best playmate and nemesis equally, as only siblings can be to each other. And she was still in the living room, sleeping innocently on the floor. I sat up, suddenly certain of one thing. He would get her. This realization sent me into action. Wearily I climbed out of the safety of my closet and went back into the living room.

The furnace had kicked back on, humming and sending eerie shadow dancers around the room. I sat down in my spot between the chair and my little sister and waited, my heart beating wildly in my chest. When he motioned for me to go with him to the bathroom, I rose dutifully and followed.

This time, it hurt.

PART ONE:

Big Sister

Chapter One

THE RACE IS ON

THE ABSOLUTE WORST PLACE YOU can live when you are kids in rural Minnesota is near your bus driver. He starts his route near his home, which means he picks you up first, drives the meandering route around at least half of the ten thousand lakes your home state is famous for, and drops you off at school an hour and a half later. You are the kids who get up while it's still dark, bundle up, trudge through the snow down the half-mile-long driveway, and stand shivering in the toolshed near the road, set up as a windbreak.

True, you are the kids who get first pick of seats, and if you are smart you will pick the one with the heater at your feet. True, you never have to ask someone to "scootch over" or get tripped by a laughing bully as you pass, searching for an opening. True, you get to influence which radio station the bus driver puts on, have a lot of time to read and talk with friends, and generally don't have to worry about the bus driver being late as you stand there at the bus stop with your teeth chattering, wondering at the numbness in your extremities and warding off frostbite with sheer Scandinavian willpower.

But you are also the kids who smell the bus the longest. You are the kids who never miss a vomiting. You are the kids who get incredibly bored, especially when your friends have already been taken home at the end of the school day. And you are the kids who make the long walk back down the driveway in ethereal dusk, day after day after day, because by virtue of living nearest your bus driver, you are also the kids who are the last to be dropped off.

So you make a game of it. It becomes a race. The first one home wins TV rights, even though Tom and Jerry is the only thing on the one channel that the scratchy black and white TV brings in. More importantly, in the sibling grand scheme of things, the first one home wins bragging rights.

When my sister and I raced it was almost accidental. "Ready, set, go!" one of us would yell and take off. My backpack, laden with books and glowing report cards from adoring teachers, bounced wildly as I ran. Hers, if she had it at all, was always light and nearly empty save for a few notebook pages of doodles she'd been working on or a note from her teacher reminding her family of her endless potential and lack of initiative. Yet somehow I pulled off the win every single time, at least in my memory. Even when we pretended not to care.

"Ready, set, go!" I'd yell.

"I'm not racing!" she'd reply indignantly, but her pace would quicken a bit.

"Me either!" I'd step faster, she'd speed up, I'd trot, she'd break into a sprint, and I'd smirk at her as I made a big show of opening the door for her to sullenly pass through. "What took you so long?"

"I wasn't racing," she'd mumble. Ours had always been a relationship balanced between competition and companionship, perfectly represented years ago by a condiment fight in my dad's old pickup when we were little. My sister and I vied for his attention in very different ways. I tried to impress and she tried to shock. I read a lot and used intelligent words like "realize" and "perpetual." She picked fights with the neighbor boys and cussed. I lectured her and she slugged me. She thought I was bossy, I told her over and over that I was not and to stop saying that and she'd better go clean up her room.

The cab of the truck was large and roomy. A long-shafted stick shift stretched out of the floorboard in the center below the radio and heat controls. Its black ball knob hung over the bench seat in the coveted spot my younger sister and I fought over—next to our dad. We had to move our legs out of the way of reverse when he shifted. It made us giggle when he bumped our knees, so he exaggerated it with a whack and a fake apology, "Sorry about that." Smack, "Oops, I apologize. I am so clumsy today." Flick, "That was totally an accident. I mean it this time." Today it was my spot, only because he'd carried her out to the truck while I ran and jumped in ahead of them.

"No fair!" she'd yelled.

"Well, you got a piggy-back ride!" I'd retorted.

"Then I get the middle next time!" she said. Satisfied, we sat back as Dad turned on the engine.

We loved his games. He was a "pull my finger" type dad, and we quickly learned not to. We also learned that the finger wasn't necessary; the imaginary duck would quack regardless of our efforts.

He'd take hold of our own hand and hit our face gently with it, "Stop hitting yourself." He'd taught us to shoot popcorn kernels at each other out of our nostrils. He'd hold our hands and feet together with one strong hand and tickle us until we cried or threatened to pee ourselves.

My dad once snuck into the bathroom where I had fallen asleep on the toilet and dropped the body of our pet canary in behind me. It had died earlier that day. Excitedly, I ran out to tell my parents, "I pooped a bird! I pooped a bird!" This is still the most embarrassing story my family likes telling strangers about me and the reason why to this day I look before I flush.

Bob Seger's raspy voice played on the radio. My dad sang along and we tried to. "Like a rock, I was strong as I could be...nothing ever got to me...I was something to see, like a rock." My dad was. Muscular and handsome, fearless and strong—I knew he was the toughest man alive. I studied his face in the rear-view mirror. His brown mustache made handlebars like the ones on his '69 Chopper. His unwashed, uncombed brown hair stuck out the sides of the black stocking cap pulled absently over his head.

"Hand me my smokes, would ya?" My sister scrambled to grab his red Marlboro pack from the passenger corner of the windshield where it had slid to a stop after a quick left turn. He pulled the last cigarette out and crushed the box into a little ball, which he threw into the pile of trash on the floor. I watched it bounce off his brown work glove and join the haphazard pile of Mountain Dew cans, sparkplugs and a couple of old, greasy white socks. His black leather jacket creaked in the cold air of the truck when he reached to light his cigarette with the dashboard lighter. His fingers and fingernails were blackened by motor oil and dirt—the permanent residual stain of a working man's hands.

My dad worked harder than anyone I knew. He built silos and fixed farm equipment all day long, then worked on motorcycles and other vehicles every night and all weekend. It didn't matter if he'd ever seen the machinery in question before; armed with a wrench, hammer and roll of duct tape, he could fix anything. I'd seen him countless times perched inside the open hood of his '66 Chevy truck or underneath someone's car in every kind of weather, tinkering, replacing, cussing and chain-smoking until the job was done. Then he'd be on to the next one.

When he sat down to watch TV or to listen to us read a story to him, he invariably fell instantly asleep. These were the days before the term "workaholic" was used. The fact that my dad could outwork anyone was not seen as a weakness but as something to be proud of. I was.

But I'd also seen another side to my dad, and as I stared at my reflection next to him in the rearview mirror, I double-checked to make sure my hands were both in my lap. I remembered all too well the stern face of my dad in that same mirror once. I had absently stuck my thumb in my mouth and he'd caught me. His glowering look scared me into pulling it out immediately and I'd vowed to never put it back in.

I'd seen my dad angry before. Once we entered the house and discovered our dog had chewed up his new stereo speakers. It yelped loudly at first as my dad cussed and screamed at it, kicking it mercilessly in the stomach. Then it was silent.

Another time it was my mom who bore the brunt of his big, heavy, angry boots. She whimpered and rolled into a fetal position until his anger was spent. Not long after, my godmother helped my mom and us kids sneak out of our house after he'd gone to work and moved us into a domestic violence shelter.

Now I was aware of my actions, and after our weekend with Dad, as we drove back toward the farmhouse mom had rented, I was taking no chances. Dad pulled into a strange driveway and told us, "Sit tight, I'll be right back. I got a buddy who owes me some money in here." I watched him walk up to the door, saw the front curtains in the window part a bit, and the front door opened quickly for him to enter. I wondered who lived inside the darkened house. Whenever my dad made these pit-stops it seemed to take forever. Parents running quick errands while kids wait in the vehicle can be a very dangerous thing. Especially if the vehicle has a stash of ketchup and mustard packets in the glove box.

I opened a ketchup and ate it. My sister opened a ketchup and drizzled it down the sides of her mouth, "Look, I'm a vampire. I vant to suck your blood!"

I opened a mustard and dabbed it under my nose. "I have a cold!"

"Yum, snot!" She reached out and touched it, then licked it off her finger.

"Ewww!" We both laughed.

My sister suddenly grabbed a mustard and smashed it between her hands, squirting it everywhere. Amidst uncontrollable giggles I grabbed a ketchup and sent it out in an explosion of red tomato droplets. Soon red and yellow blobs covered the cab of the truck, slid gloopingly down the windows and splattered our faces. We were so caught up in our Jackson Pollock moment that we didn't notice Dad had come back until the truck door suddenly flung open.

"What the hell's going on in here?" There we were, covered in condiments, eyes wide. His scowl slid into a smile, which my sister took as permission to send another mustard packet flying. I told her to stop. Dad grabbed a rag and wiped off our faces. I used an old sock from the floor to try and clean it up the best I could, but it mostly just smeared into the fabric.

"She started it! I told her to stop!" I blurted, worried that Dad would be mad at me for letting my sister get so wild in the first place and for making such a big mess.

"So! It was fun!" she replied.

"Don't worry about it, honey. This old truck needed some decoration!" Then he reached over and tousled my sister's hair and chuckled, "You come by it honestly, kid."

We rode along in silence, mesmerized by the windshield wipers pushing the snowflakes across the wide window in front of us. Silhouetted against a darkening sky, they would pile up and be whisked away again and again. The heat was turned on full blast but was no match for the immense truck cab, filled with a bitter Minnesota chill. It seeped in through every rusted hole in the floorboard and wrapped its clammy hands around our feet. It whistled through the little triangular glass next to the passenger side window and bit at our ears. Where my dad's window was cracked open a couple inches to let the cigarette smoke out, it sent in sneaky tendrils of cold air that flicked at our exposed noses. Dad reached behind the seat and pulled out an old gray woolen blanket as he asked, "Cold?" We huddled under it, close together.

After a few miles I felt my sister slump against my shoulder, asleep. I tucked the blanket around her and worked up the nerve to break the silence. "Dad?"

He took one last drag off his smoke, pushed it out the window and rolled the window up. Then he put his arm around my shoulder and glanced at me in the rear-view mirror. "Yeah, baby?"

"Are you coming to get us next weekend?"

"I told you I would. How about we go get pizza and feed the ducks again. Crazy ducks, don't even know they're supposed to fly south for winter. Of course, if I had a warm pond to live in and people came and fed me, I'd stick around, too. Hey! That's a great idea! I can get a big duck suit, you know? And just go live at the pond and your sister and you can come feed me from time to time. Then, when I see a good looking woman I can go squawking after her! Quack! Quack!" He laughed and I joined in. The dubious little rock inside my stomach and I hoped he was serious—about his coming next weekend.

We turned left onto the gravel road and passed the little white church on the corner where my sister and I had ridden our bikes to Vacation Bible School the previous summer.

One of those mornings I'd run over a snake. During the entire ride to the church, I imagined its wriggling body making its way around my tire spokes, over my fender and up my seat as I pedaled madly, holding in screams. I was too afraid to stop, too afraid to slow down and too afraid to look back. I knew it was going to sink its fangs into the back of my neck at any moment. When I got to the church, I kept pumping my legs across the yard before I dumped my bike in the grass. I was all the way into the building before I could shake the feeling of the horrible thing chasing me. My sister just pulled in coolly beside me and laughed, "Fraidy cat!"

The memory sent a shudder through my already chilled body. Dad rubbed my arm briskly before reaching down to downshift the truck. His right-hand turn meant we were home. The blue light of the TV danced through the living room window. Mom was looking out, waving and smiling. Dad pulled in beside the bee tree, and I was glad it was winter. No one ever parked there in the summer—well, not more than once anyway. In warm weather, hundreds of bees swarmed to its blossoms, making a loud, droning buzz. More than one visitor had been stung in the months we'd lived there.

I was pretty sure my sister had woken up when we'd pulled onto the bumpy gravel road, but she pretended to sleep now. My dad scooped her up and took her inside. I followed behind, carrying our little duffel bag full of the clothes and things we'd brought with us for the weekend. Over his shoulder, she opened one eye and stuck out her tongue at me. I stuck mine out at her and kept walking, lost in my own thoughts.

When Dad put her down on the couch, she pretended to wake up. "Daddy, don't go!"

"I'll be back next weekend, Squirt, I promise! I love you."

My mom had to hold her so she wouldn't follow him out the door. He hugged me and told me he loved me and he'd see me next weekend. "I love you, too, Dad. Thanks for a fun weekend. I'll, uh, see you later."

Then he was gone. He hopped into his truck and it roared backward out of the driveway. I heard two things: my sister's loud wails and him driving away. I turned to go unpack our things.

The next weekend found us looking out the window expectantly at the appointed time, my sister excited because it was her turn to have the middle seat. Seeing no one, we went out to the front step. Hours went by and we sat by the road, willing every car that went by to be his. After dark, our mom gently made us come in. She told us that something must have come up and that he wasn't going to make it that night. She hugged us close, wiped away our tears and tucked us tenderly into our beds.

When my sister asked if she could sleep with me that night, I pulled the blanket over us and held her close. I fell asleep to the sound of quiet, breath-hitching sobs. I wasn't sure which were hers and which were mine. And in the back of my mind echoed the sound of his grumbly old truck, quickly driving away from us.

It would be many years before he returned.

Chapter Two

SO UGLY THEY'RE CUTE

MY GRANDMOTHER LOVED ME. I knew this with an unshakable certainty. My earliest positive memories all include her. We spent many weekends in the safety of her trailer. Here Grandma and our loving aunts tended to us. They bathed and gently nursed our physical signs of neglect, our bloody diaper rashes, growling tummies and dirty clothing. Grandma's lap was the only place I always felt safe, wanted and loved. The moments I spent in it, munching on popcorn and watching TV, were the only times I ever felt at peace. The hours she spent teaching me to braid, cooking with me, listening to me read to her, and telling me about the love of Jesus were the best moments of my young life.

But Grandma moved away. With her she took any hope of respite, and our isolation was complete. I devoured her letters, her faithful birthday cards, and the religious tracts and poems she enclosed. The light she shone in our darkness transcended the miles and years. I missed her terribly, but I always knew my grandmother loved me. She was one of the first, but by no means the last to do so.

In the year 1983, I figured out the only two things I

have ever really needed to know. The first was the certainty of my own poverty. The second was that there is always hope. Both these lessons were crystallized by a consumer-driven, maniacal craze over a doll.

I didn't even like dolls, unless they were the somewhat anatomically correct kind. We had "Wild Haircut" Barbies and "Can't Get His Tight Plastic Boots Back On" Kens who invariably wound up in compromising positions through no fault of our own. Take any naked dolls and throw them together into a bag, under a bed or in the backseat of a car, and the inevitable result will always be the same. Little plastic limbs will entwine. Hard little bodies will be pressed together in inappropriate places, and third-graders like me will have to decide whether to intrude on these private moments or apologize and slowly close the door.

Baby dolls held no appeal for me, probably because I had real baby sisters whom I cared for from my earliest memories. These were my beloved little dolls whom I changed, fed, burped and played with.

Then along came the Cabbage Patch Kids. I looked up from playing with Star Wars figures long enough to realize that every girl in my school wanted one. I eavesdropped from the tree I'd climbed on the playground as they talked about how wonderful these dolls were. I listened from behind my books on the school bus as they planned and plotted, dreaming about Christmas break and how they were sure that they knew what would be under the tree waiting for them. Suddenly, despite my tomboy tendencies, with my entire being, I wanted one too.

My sister and I knew we wanted ones who looked just like us, which meant that along with having blue eyes, mine would have brown hair and hers would have yellow. We knew they would sleep with us and go wherever we went. We knew they'd be sisters and share clothing and play together. The only thing we weren't sure about was whether or not they would ever actually be ours.

We'd overheard adults talking about how expensive and difficult the dolls were to get. We'd watched the news where parents lined up outside stores and then rioted, angrily snatching dolls out of other people's hands. We didn't even know where those stores were but figured it was probably in the cities somewhere since the stores nearest to us carried only groceries, beer and bait.

These should have been our red flags, but fueled by the shows we watched about endless Christmas miracles and our own blissful ignorance about finances, we asked, begged, and bargained with our mom to get them for us. We asked, begged, and bargained with Santa to get them for us. We asked, begged, and bargained with God himself to get them for us. Having done all we could do for almost four months to influence our fate, we went to bed on Christmas Eve, naively confident that there would be two boxes under the tree with our names on them and our newly adopted kids inside.

Mom always did everything she could to make Christmas wonderful. She was very artistic and creative, helping us decorate the tree with a variety of ornaments and homemade garland. We strung popcorn and sprinkled glitter onto our cutout paper balls while we watched every

Christmas special that came on TV. The break from school meant going sledding and playing board games with Mom and each other. Best of all was the Christmas dinner feast of delicious food she'd spent months saving for and hours cooking: ham, turkey, stuffing, potatoes, beans, rolls and pies. It was a treat to eat so well so far into the month; it was our own version of a Christmas miracle.

On Christmas Eve we'd gather around while she read *'Twas the Night Before Christmas,* then she'd tuck us in and gently remind us that Santa couldn't come until we were all asleep. Before long her voice would rise in response to our giggling and talking in bed and her gentle reminder became a threat. We'd turn on each other then. "You better be quiet or Santa won't come!" We'd freeze, unmoving under our blankets, pressing our lips together to keep from talking. No one wanted to be responsible for that!

He always did come. In the morning, under the tree we discovered that he'd brought a new sled and mittens and hats. Inside our hanging stockings, he'd left candy canes and Hershey's kisses. And later that day, a police officer brought him in a squad car with a big black garbage bag full of Toys for Tots. Inside were puzzles, games and new Barbie dolls. There were cheap little cameras, watches, stuffed animals and plastic jewelry. He brought us socks, underwear and new sweaters. But he never did bring a Cabbage Patch Kid. Not to us.

I began to think hard about the matter then. It was my first inkling that there must be more to receiving good gifts than being naughty or nice, because everybody knew I was nice and my sister was naughty, yet neither of us had gotten what we'd asked for. I realized that neither my parents, Santa nor God were magical genies who would respond to my whims. I recognized my mom's limitations, decided Santa couldn't be trusted, and was completely confused about who God was. Then again, aside from Grandma's pamphlets and childhood words spoken over me, we had just recently been introduced.

Our family moved into a rental which was a kid's dream come true. The house was huge, both levels were separate apartments, and one of my best friends from school lived downstairs with her family. Behind the stairs we found a secret door that led to the closet in her bedroom. We knocked secret codes on her wall and held important club meetings. There was a hill to sled and ponds to skate. On Mother's Day weekend we woke to six feet of snow drifting over the yard. We had to jump off the back deck and go around the house to the front to shovel out the door, which was entirely blocked with a wall of white. We spent the next few days making tunnels and giant snowmen.

The property had once been the site of a wild animal farm. Large pens that had housed bears and foxes lined one side of the property. These were an improvement over the corn cribs of our last rental for playing jail or zoo. My sister and I spent hours climbing around them, cleaning them out, pretending to be monkeys or convicts, clinking a tin cup across the bars and calling out, "I want my phone call!"

"Be quiet in there! You'll get your phone call when I say you'll get your phone call!" I swung a ring full of old keys around on the end of a string and walked back and forth outside the front of her cell, a menacing orange cap gun stuck inside my waistband, plastic badge pinned to my shirt.

"I didn't do it, I'm innocent!"

"Yeah, that's what they all say. But we've got tons of evidence. You tell us who you're working for and we might let you off."

"I ain't no snitch! Get outta here, copper! I want my lawyer! And a peanut butter jelly sandwich!"

We had watched enough TV to be experts on the law. Knowing she was entitled to lunch, I walked to the house to make her some food, but not without tossing back, "You'll eat what I tell you to eat, you dirty rat!"

I brought out a sleeve of saltines and a jar of peanut butter, joining her in her cell. We sat on a couple of old overturned buckets and munched in silence for a few minutes before she spoke up. "What do you think it's really like to be in jail?"

"I don't know. Probably pretty boring, I guess. I wouldn't like to be locked up all the time, that's for sure."

"Me neither. I'd just escape, though."

"No you wouldn't. You can't escape from everything, you know. Some things are too strong for you."

"Whatever! I could too escape! Watch me!" Before I could stop her she ran over to the big iron door and swung it shut tightly. The old rusty latch on the outside closed with a loud click.

"What'd you do that for? Now how are we going to get out?" I tried to swallow my panic along with the half-chewed bite of crackers in my mouth. I knew from experience that the rusted, heavy latch was difficult to open; I had needed to use a screwdriver and a hammer to get it open in the first place.

"Easy! I'll just reach out of the bars and open it from the outside, like this!" She reached through and fidgeted with the lock. She shook it and punched at it with her fist. She looked at me helplessly. "It's stuck, you try!"

I walked over, angrily claustrophobic now, and tried to manipulate the mechanism, but the weight of the door had wedged the latch shut, and even with both of us pushing, pulling and hitting at the lock, we were unable to budge it. My sister climbed to the top of the cage and yelled, "Help, get us out of here! We're trapped!"

Unfortunately, that's what we always yelled when we pretended to be recently captured wild beasts or ruthless mobsters locked up for our own good or the good of society. If Mom heard, she didn't come running, but our neighbor did.

We'd met him when we first moved in; he and his wife lived next door to the west. They invited us to the church he pastored and told us we could ride with their family. Mom wasn't interested in going, but we were. We both loved it from the start. People were kind to us, we played fun games, ate snacks and did Bible activities. It was an entirely different culture from the way I had grown up. Up to that point, other than at the VBS we'd crashed the summer before and our Grandma's soft-spoken Bible stories, we'd only heard the name of God in very special circumstances, like when someone was putting out curtain fires, "Well, Je-zus Chryst, why on earth would you be playing with my lighter in the first place?" Or if they'd run out of beer, "Goddammit! The keg's empty!"

The tall, smiling pastor opened the gate for us, "You girls okay?"

"Yep, Pastor, fine," my sister bounded off to find the next adventure. I walked back to the house next to him.

"Thanks for helping us out." I looked gratefully up into his kind face.

"No problem. How's school going?"

"Pretty good. I love my teacher! She's really funny and she goes on all these adventures, like she travelled to the Galapagos Islands and showed us all these pictures. And she's gonna go to the Olympics! When I grow up I want to have lots of adventures like her!"

Pastor smiled, "Wow, those are a lot of adventures! You know, living life with God is full of adventure, too. I've sure never gotten bored!" He looked closely at me then. "How's your mom? Is she feeling better?"

"Um, sure. She's doing fine. But she is too busy with the babies to go to church with us." I wasn't even sure why I made excuses for her. It just came naturally. I wanted him to like us, to like her. I didn't want to disappoint.

"Okay. Well, she is always welcome to come, of course. We'd love to have her and your younger sisters, too." We'd reached my front door. "See you Sunday?"

I smiled, "Yep. See you Sunday." But by Saturday we'd moved thirty miles away with Mom's boyfriend. We had no way to tell the pastor where we'd gone.

A couple of weeks later a silver car pulled into our driveway. An older man and woman walked up to our door and introduced themselves. They were friends with our pastor neighbor who'd apparently asked around about us. This nice couple pastored their own church nearby. They began to pick us up faithfully each week. This church was much smaller and didn't have many children, but that just made us the center of attention to a congregation of doting grandparents. We loved it! Our Sunday school teacher encouraged Bible memorization, rewarding us with candy bars. My sister and I would stand in front of the congregation and recite entire chapters. "The Lord is my shepherd, I shall not want. He makes me lie down in green pastures, He leads me beside the still waters. He restores my soul…" Sometimes the pastor and his wife would take us to lunch at a local diner afterwards. This was a huge treat for us as our family's version of eating out was grilling venison burgers in the backyard.

Every week my Sunday school teacher would tell us that the only way to heaven was by accepting Jesus as our Savior, that He wanted to be our best friend and give us peace in our heart. Every week she asked if we were ready to invite Him into our hearts and be saved. Every week my sister would say, "No," and I would say, "Not yet." I wasn't sure what I was waiting for. It sounded pretty good to me, but I was still observing and thinking, processing who God was and what He had to do with me.

One day after the service was over, we walked out to the car, ready for the pastor and his wife to take us home. A few other women followed us out. The adults stood there beaming as my sister and I opened the rear doors. My sister gasped, "Oh my God!" and reached in quickly to unstrap the seatbelt.

I stood, shocked and staring. There she sat in my seat, a miniature version of me in blue jeans and a little green t-shirt. She had long brown braided yarn hair and blue painted eyes, and her wide smile matched mine. I reached in and pulled her out to hug her close. Tears of gratitude filled my eyes as I gave hugs to these women who'd sacrificed their time, money and talents to painstakingly sew Cabbage Patch dolls for my sister and me. They were so well done that I didn't know they were homemade unless I looked for the signature on the bum. I didn't care that she wasn't store-bought—she was mine. My sister loved hers, too, and we played endlessly with our little look-alike daughters.

Now I knew with certainty that receiving good gifts had nothing at all to do with deserving them. It had everything to do with the ability and benevolence of the giver.

That summer an anonymous donor paid our way to Bible camp. On the first night a special preacher was coming to speak. It turned out to be our pastor, the one from the little church we went to. At the end of the first night he gave an invitation to come forward and accept Jesus, and my heart started racing. I felt a deep longing bubble up from my soul. It propelled my legs with urgency to the front altar as quickly as they would move. Tears of relief and hope and love and wonder and joy and sorrow ran down my face, and I sobbed as I opened my heart fully to God. When I stood up, it was with an altogether unfamiliar sensation spreading through my body from the inside out. It was peace. Peace like I'd only ever found on my grandma's lap so many years ago.

My pastor and my Sunday school teacher both hugged me, tears in their own eyes. I think they knew how important this decision would be for the rest of my life. I couldn't wait to write my grandma with the good news. She was really excited and told me how proud she was of me and happy that I'd committed my life to Jesus.

But as I entered my teens, I all but forgot about it. Two things happened that pushed it to the back of my mind. The first was that our little church decided to close its doors due to lack of finances. The second was that we moved again. This time it was into town, and my sister and I continued our quest for adventure—but in partying, instead of childish pursuits like playing with dolls. When church folks called to ask if we wanted a ride to a nearby church, we gave excuses. We were needed at home, we were busy, or we just couldn't make it this week. Eventually they took the hint and stopped asking. They told us to call them when we were ready. And when Grandma's letters came faithfully each birthday, I threw away the little enclosed Gospel tracts without reading them. I instead embraced the life of alcohol and sex that was more familiar to me— my family legacy.

Years later, when I was reunited with some of these beloved people, I learned that even though we'd moved around often enough to lose touch altogether, neither our church friends nor my grandmother had ever forgotten about us. They had never stopped praying for or asking about us. We were the granddaughters of a woman who fasted and prayed zealously for our salvation. We were the two sisters in worn hand-me-downs, tangled hair, muddy shoes and secondhand smoke smell, bickering in the backseat and eagerly riding to church week after week. We were often hungry physically, but they saw another, deeper, love hunger, and fed it, too.

Chapter Three

TOO MUCH BLUE

SLOWLY I TURNED THE PIECE in my hand, trying to figure out which way was up or down or sideways, searching hopefully for any irregularity or distinction in shape, shade or size that would give me a clue as to where it belonged. Frustrated, I tossed it back into the box with its identical cousins and got up to get a drink.

Kool-Aid, red and cold from the pitcher, poured into my metal glass. With the first sip I knew my sister had made this batch. I always added the one-quarter cup of sugar directed on the package, but she always quadrupled it. I poured a cup for her, too.

The house was quiet; our younger sisters were asleep upstairs. I joined my sister in the living room, pushed an overflowing ashtray over and set our drinks on the coffee table.

"Thanks," she absently said, concentrating on the drawing in her lap. The TV was on low, taking the edge off the silence of the house, keeping our underlying fears at bay. She was playing her favorite movie for at least the tenth time this week. I stood watching Julia Roberts get asked to leave a posh clothing store before I sat down on the couch and peered at the notebook in my sister's lap.

"What are you drawing?"

"Nothing, just goofing around." She flipped it over self-consciously to hide it from me.

"Let me see."

"Fine!" and shoved it into my lap. She sipped her Kool-Aid, pretending not to care about my reaction.

Doodles nearly filled the margins—swirls, crosses, hearts and the name of her boyfriend in block lettering and other scripts ten different ways. In the center of the page she'd drawn a large sun. Inside the sun there was a hand holding onto a star.

"This is really good! What's it for?"

Her face relaxed from a guarded scowl into a small, proud smile at the compliment. "It's just an idea I have for a tattoo."

"What's it mean?"

"Just, you know, gripping the light, I guess."

"This is really cool!

We sat together watching Vivian march back into the store to ask the sales clerk, "You work on commission, right?" We spoke the next lines in unison, "Big mistake... big, big mistake!"

We watched the shopping spree a bit longer before I asked, "Hey, do you want to work the puzzle with me?"

"Sure," my sister shrugged. We moved to the dining room table and pored over the pieces for a minute in silence. "All that's left is blue!"

"I know."

"That sucks. Why don't we just start a new one?"

"This one's not done yet."

"So! I quit." She went back to her notebook on the couch.

I became lost again in the sky and sea of this other place, far away and beautiful and so very, very blue.

"Bars are almost closed," she said.

Glancing up at the clock, I read 12:45, "Yep, she should be coming home soon."

"She better bring me a Dew like I asked her to."

"Call and remind her."

She turned the rotary phone wheel quickly and impatiently waited in-between numbers for it to click back to start. We both knew the numbers of all the bars in town by heart, and the bartenders recognized our voices. "My mom there?" She got a yes from the third bar and absently twisted the phone cord in her finger while she waited for Mom to come to the phone. We both heard through the receiver, "It's your damn kids calling again!" as we gave our middle fingers to the phone and giggled.

Her slurred voice came on the line, "Hi, hunnney. I'm on mmmy way home. I jes ran into an ol friend. I haven't seen her in years. We've been catching up and I been telling her how wonderful my kids are. I'm sssso proud of you. I tolll her how you got student of the week."

"Mom, it's your other daughter. Are you gonna bring me a pop?"

"Oh, hi. Yeah, I didn't forget. I've got it right here. You wannnted a MountnnDew, rrright? I'll bbbring it with mmme, okay. I'm on my way home. I ran into a friend I used to go to school with. I haven't seenner in years. I was telling her how you were on the honor roll..."

"That wasn't me. Whatever. See you soon, Mom."

She hung up and we both rolled our eyes. "You got any smokes?"

"Yep, I stole a pack yesterday," I told her.

"Half are mine then, or I'll tell."

"Fine, they're up in my sock drawer. Don't wake up the kids."

She returned a few minutes later and handed me a cigarette. She went back to her movie and we smoked and waited in silence.

Hours later I'd put the last blue pieces to rest. Relief flooded through me as I finally heard Mom pull into the driveway. It felt like we had just gotten a breath of fresh air, without realizing we'd been holding it. We walked her in and helped her to bed. "You go to bed kids, it's a school night. I don't know why you're up so late."

I lay in my bed staring up at the ceiling. Like so many nights before, unprovoked tears came, and though I tried to cry silently, my sister always heard. "Move over!" she gruffly ordered. Then she gently lay next to me and put her arms around me while I sobbed into her shoulder, and she into mine. Exhaustion drying our tears, we wiped our snotty noses on the blanket and lay there without talking.

Just as I was drifting off to sleep her voice cut through the silence, "Shit!"

"What?"

"She forgot my damn pop!" In the darkness we laughed until our stomachs hurt.

After school the next day, we got the announcement

from Mom, still hungover. Social Services was coming Monday. The weekend became a flurry of activity in preparation. We knew the drill—clean up the house, keep the secrets, downplay the drama, and make sure to say what they need to hear. With any luck they wouldn't be back until next year when some other concerned citizen, family member or school official made inquiries. Then they'd call again and tell us when they'd be coming for a visit, and the process would be repeated.

Getting the house in order was no easy task. The laundry of four kids and one adult was piled up on the bathroom floor, waiting to be bagged up and brought to the laundromat. Since we'd moved back into a farmhouse in the country, this usually happened once a month, depending on whether we had the quarters, gas money and time to do it. There the heap sat, growing slowly with the pieces of our shabby wardrobes that actually made it from the musty piles on our bedroom floors downstairs to their designated spot. It became a larger hill with the bedding and blankets soiled by our pets or ourselves. The hill became a mountain from our annual lice infestation.

We would pack it all into big black plastic bags and load it into our old orange station wagon. We would drive the ten miles into town and park behind the laundromat. We would spend the day washing, drying, folding and amusing ourselves. We would race the laundry carts, play hide-and-go-seek, and beg Mom for change to buy snacks at the gas station. We would watch CBS, the only channel we'd watched for years, on the old snowy black and white TV. Some people in town had cable, some in the country had giant, round satellites that filled up their front yards, and some had gaudy looking antennas sticking out the roofs of their houses, strapped to their chimneys or supported by bent, rusty poles. We had a set of rabbit ears poking up, cockeyed and eager. Once in a while, they could also get us a static-filled picture of PBS, which we didn't appreciate.

The laundromat also had an ancient Centipede game against one wall, which got its share of use and abuse. Some older kids, whose hands were too big to do it for themselves, showed us how to pop open the front compartment far enough to wedge our smaller hands inside and press the little red button to get free games. If we did it for them, they let us play once or twice. This arrangement was great for us because we certainly didn't have any extra quarters.

With the laundry accomplished, we would return home to tackle the other rooms in the house. The kitchen, living room and eating area would get picked up, scrubbed and put into order. We would all work on our own bedrooms. Mom's was downstairs and all four of us kids slept upstairs. We had a long attic with a sloped, pointed ceiling. My sister and I were on one side, and the babies were on the other. Invariably, we would make numerous trips downstairs to tell on the others, what they were or weren't doing, until my mom would tell us not to come down again until our rooms were clean. Then we would just yelled downstairs.

A one hour job stretched into at least five. We would find things we thought were gone forever. We would creatively rearrange our few items of furniture in order to make it seem like we had new rooms. We would be grossed out many times by what we found underneath our beds or clothes. We would renew our vows to never again repeat the sniff test. Most importantly, we would finish the overwhelming task set before us.

Mom, meanwhile, had aired out the house, thrown a roast in the oven and deep-cleaned. Carpets were vacuumed, floors scrubbed, and cupboards stocked, we were ready for anything—a blizzard, nuclear war, possibly even a visit from the state.

At dinner, our coaching was completed. We all sat down to our meal as if that were a nightly occurrence. We ate together, said please and thank you, and talked about school. After we'd done the supper dishes, we sat around and played board games together. We laughed and felt normal, like a family. Mom told us that this was the way it was going to be from now on, and we believed her. It seemed to erase the pain of the many nights when she hadn't been there, when we'd fended for ourselves with few groceries and no idea when or in what condition she'd be coming home.

Together we watched TV, and then Mom tucked us into bed. I fell asleep feeling secure and hopeful and happy. Our morning consisted of cheerful greetings, a warm breakfast, and a pleasant, peaceful Sunday together. We liked this reality and believed with all the power of our short-term memories that this would indeed be our lives from now on. And because we were in this new start, there was no reason to bring up the past, we reasoned.

The next morning we watched a newer model silver sedan pull into our long driveway, crunching gravel slowly underneath its tires. It sidled up next to our old, rusted orange station wagon and parked. We sat properly in our clean clothes, bathed and groomed. The TV was off, and I was reading books to the baby in my lap while my sister was playing a game with the toddler. We were anxious because a lot was riding on this visit, but we were ready.

We peeked out the window curiously at the State Lady as her short, nylon covered legs stepped out of the car door, wind picking up and swirling snow eddies around her ankles, making her long skirt dance. Her hair blew around wildly except what was plastered to her head with hair spray. She adjusted her long black wool coat and swept her grey scarf around her neck. Her hand maintained contact with the car to steady herself on the icy tire ruts as she carefully shuffle-stepped to the trunk to retrieve her black attaché case. We watched her from the window as she took those same experienced, almost skating, steps across the frozen ground to our front stoop and knocked. We looked at each other with an unspoken "Places!" command and hurried to our spots as Mom cordially opened the door.

Our State Lady seemed caring and kind—but we knew better. We stayed on guard as she waltzed into the room, eyes surveying every detail, looking for any excuse to tear apart our family unit. She asked if she could see each room in the house, and of course my mom complied cheerfully. The tour began, my mom leading the way. State Lady took notes and asked lots of questions while four curious kids followed behind. She looked into the cupboards and refrigerator, noting the kitchen stocked neatly with food and countertops wiped clean.

She commented on how cozy our living room was and

how pretty Mom's plants were. She looked around the bathroom and my mom's room quickly. Seemingly satisfied with the lower level, she asked where our kid rooms were and asked for us to take her there so she could have a talk with us alone, without our mom.

Once upstairs, she sat on my sister's bed and asked politely about some of our toys, the Santa bear we'd gotten from the cops' Santa program, and the poster of Tom Cruise on my wall. She admired the ribbons and certificates of achievement I'd tacked up all over my wood panel walls. The two younger kids played with their toys and brought us books to read to them while we talked about school and home and Mom and discipline and who cooked and cleaned and safety and how absolutely normal and happy and perfect our little family was.

When she left, she was smiling. We knew we'd done it. We'd beat the system again.

As soon as the silver car left the end of the driveway, Mom cussed loudly about the state's interference while she changed her clothes and put on her shoes. She told us that she was going to run into town quick for a pack of cigarettes and that she'd be right back.

After we'd given them dinner and put the younger kids to bed, I sat down at the kitchen table. My sister brought her drawing tablet over and plopped down across from me. "You want some Kool-Aid?"

"It's gone."

"I'll make more."

"Just use a quarter cup of sugar."

"That's nasty. I always do a cup."

"I know," and I grabbed a steak knife to carefully cut open a new puzzle.

Chapter Four

STINGS LIKE A CATERPILLAR

In college, my favorite place to study was under a large oak tree on campus. I'd sit with my back resting against the rough trunk, listening to the gentle shushing sound of the new green leaves in the canopy above. I enjoyed the intermittent distractions of squirrels playing tag along the ground and in the branches above my head. Spring showers had finally given way to sunshine, and I was soaking it up.

I squinted hard at the psychology book resting on my legs and highlighted a few lines. *Dissociation is a term in psychology describing a wide array of experiences from mild detachment from immediate surroundings to more severe detachment from physical and emotional experience. It is commonly displayed on a continuum.* It was another few pages before I realized I wasn't retaining anything I'd read, that my mind was drifting again and again to the phone call.

It had come at three a.m. The women's dorm had a payphone on the first floor. When it rang, whoever answered it would go get the person it was for or leave a message on the whiteboard outside her door if she couldn't be found. But this was unnecessary protocol on the night my sister called because I was up, restless without reason. I heard it ring, shattering the silence of the peaceful dormitory, and ran from my room down the hall to answer.

"Hello?"

"Hey, it's me."

I sat down, suddenly breathless. "Are you okay, little sis?"

"Oh yeah, I'm fine. Just called to talk. How's school going?"

"Um, okay. I like my classes, except some are really early in the morning. I might not have come here if I'd known I'd have class at seven-fifteen."

She laughed. "I got your letter. Did you really quit smoking?"

Smiling at the memory, I told her, "Yup. The day I came on campus. Dad and I drove around town for hours so I could smoke 'just one more.' Are you sure you're okay? Do you need a bus ticket home?"

"Oh no. I'm doing fine here. Got a job and place to stay and everything. Have you talked to Mom and Dad?"

"Yes, and they're worried about you, too. Please come home."

"I'm fine, really. Listen, I gotta go, but give everyone my love. I love you, big sis!"

"I love you, too, little sis!" I heard a click, and then she was gone.

She had run away for the millionth time since I had moved in with my stepfather. He had been a big influence on Mom's sobriety. When she relapsed and moved out, I was given the option of staying with him and finishing my junior and senior years of high school in relative stability, or continuing in the chaos that is life with addiction. The right choice was not the easy choice because it divided our family. My younger sister went with Mom. I didn't know many of the details of what had happened after that because we didn't live together.

We visited a lot but were both going down very different roads. My stepdad gave me hope that I was not doomed to repeat the patterns of addiction. I went to Al-Anon/Alateen and learned to express my feelings, recognize healthy boundaries, and understand the twelve steps as a pathway to healing. My sister was still partying every chance she got and really wasn't interested in changing. Honestly, I was still partying every chance I got too, but the difference was that I really did want a different life than my default lifestyle. It was like I had gained some tools but utterly lacked the power to use them. I felt trapped.

My junior year something devastating and wonderful happened. Our house burnt to the ground. When we had lost everything and were homeless, a church stepped in. We were put up in a motel until our insurance kicked in and we could move to an apartment. They brought us clothes, toys for my baby sister and food. They spent time with us, inviting us to their homes for meals or just hanging out. I experienced it again—agape love—unselfish giving without ulterior motive or condition. These were a people who loved because Love was in them. I was hungry for more.

During my senior year I accidentally went to a Christian concert (I thought it was just going to be rock and roll), and when an invitation was given to give my life to Jesus, I felt a familiar stirring in my heart. I was so eager to be changed from the inside, and I'd been trying to find salvation through counterfeits—alcohol, my boyfriend, perfectionism. Here I was, sitting in an auditorium, tears streaming down my face as I allowed Hope, Love and Acceptance to swallow me whole. I committed to stay in this relationship for the rest of my life. I began to hang out with believers and read my Bible constantly.

I found out that I didn't need alcohol to make me feel different because I genuinely felt different after this experience of surrender. I didn't need my boyfriend to be my escape or a distraction from a troubled home life because I now felt the power and clarity of walking with a Savior who comforted and counseled me continually. I began to pray about my future direction and sensed an interest in missions work. I enrolled in Bible college and knew it was the right decision for me (despite rules about dress codes, curfews and ungodly early classes). But it meant leaving my family in the chaos, and that was almost more than I could bear, especially after my sister ran away.

On my way to Iowa I picked her up at Dad's in my old Cutlass. She had run away from Mom to live with him. I'd seen her a few months before, but just briefly. All of my rowdy family had come to graduation and my baptism. I'd emerged from the icy cold water and I saw her standing, cool and aloof. She'd thrown her cigarette butt into the sand and walked over to hug me, wet clothes and all. I couldn't put my finger on it, but something had changed in her. It felt like the distance between us could no longer be bridged by a hug.

We drove around in the heat of the late summer day reminiscing. We went to our old elementary school and walked the halls and playground. We drove through town, recalling the drive-in where we'd stood hysterically crying next to the car as we watched ET die. We stopped and got root beer floats at the A&W, then aimlessly drove out into the countryside. I passed a little white church and she said, "Stop, turn here!"

I remembered it then, too. We pulled in and sat outside the church, sipping our floats in silence. "I loved coming here. Everybody was so nice," she said.

I nodded. "I think this is the first place I started to figure out Jesus is real, you know."

She nodded. We drank the last of our root beers, seeing who could slurp hers the loudest and longest through her straw. She belched loudly and I tossed the box of Marlboro Reds at her after shaking a cigarette out. "That's a cool lighter. Who'd you steal it from?" I teased.

It had a Harley Davidson emblem. We both answered my question in unison, "Dad," then giggled. She turned the metal Zippo over and over in her hands, suddenly serious. "You want to go burn it down?"

I knew what she was talking about immediately. "Yes. But somebody probably lives there." I was only half joking.

"Let's go find out. Maybe they'll let us look around."

I started the car and we drove up the hill and around the corner. There it was, the old farmhouse of our earliest memories. We pulled in the driveway. "Hey, the bee tree is gone!" she exclaimed.

We parked, brazenly walked up the steps to the front door and knocked. A little girl peeked through the glass in the door and a woman opened the door, "Can I help you?"

"We used to live here when we were kids and we were just wondering if we could look around a bit?" I asked.

She nodded and gestured to the yard, "Sure." We walked around, remembering. The stingingly sweet scent of cow manure hung heavy in the air, just as it had when we lived there, helping to jog our memories.

"I bet there are still hornets in the hay mow. Wonder if our fort is still up in the rafters of the corn crib?" We chattered on, laughing and enjoying piecing together the details from our past at the old farm.

"Remember riding our bikes to the dairy farm and riding through the barn like we were bikers?"

"Oh, hey, remember when we almost got decapitated going under the barbed wire fence on the sled?"

"Or falling through the window off that desk?"

We laughed. "Man, I really don't know how we survived living here."

We made our way back to the front door to tell the woman we'd be on our way then. She was standing outside, holding a baby on her hip. A man had joined her, as well as the little girl we'd seen earlier. All silently watched our approach.

"Thank you so much for letting us wander around your yard," I thanked the mom and dad.

"You want to come in the house?" the mom asked.

I looked at my sister, suddenly uncertain. She nodded and shrugged, "Sure, why not?"

We walked up the cement steps and onto a dingy, dirty porch. I hesitated, "You sure?" She pushed open the door and I was immediately transported back a decade. The wallpaper, floors and grimy, painted doors were unchanged.

We talked little and in hushed tones now as we walked slowly from room to room. Her bedroom had been upstairs, so we started there. "Remember when you barged in and saw me cutting my hair? You practically flew down the steps to go tell Mom!" I forced a smile.

We peeked into the master and other smaller bedroom before heading back downstairs. I followed my sister to my old room. She rattled on about boxing in our little shorts and changing in the closet. My fake smile was now plastered on.

The carpet in the living room was the same green shag. The ancient brown furnace stood against one side of the room, tiredly waiting for fall. "Remember when you set the curtains on fire? Mom was so mad at me! Did you ever tell her it was really you playing with her lighter?"

I smirked. "Of course not."

"Jerk!" She punched my arm.

We walked to the kitchen. "We used to have so much fun sliding across this floor. Too bad I was always so much faster than you!" she baited.

"Was not!" I retorted.

"Was so!"

"Was not!"

"Whatever." We giggled.

The little girl who lived there walked past us toward a large grimy door on the other side of the kitchen. I froze, watching and silently willing her to leave it closed. But she didn't. She swung it open to reveal a filthy bathroom. My heart dropped into my feet, turning them into cement when I needed them to help me flee. Memories assaulted my senses like strobe lights.

Darkness. Yellow jammies. Darkness. Gleaming white teeth. Darkness. Orange jammies. Bloody white towel. Darkness.

My head was suddenly pounding with the onset of a migraine. These too had their beginnings in this old farmhouse. When I looked to my sister for help, I saw it in her haunted eyes as she watched the little girl walk in and close the door behind her. I suddenly knew it with certainty. He'd gotten her, too.

Blood stabbed my brain in a blinding rush of rage. My legs began to buckle. She caught me around the waist and held me up, addressing the little family who'd been following us around, "Uh, excuse us, we have to go. Thanks for letting us look around."

She led me to the car and opened the driver door for me to climb inside. I crawled into the backseat instead and buried my face in the fabric to hide from the light cutting at my eyelids. "I guess I'll drive then." She started my car and drove us far out onto a country road before turning off into an abandoned driveway and parking under a shady tree.

I sat up groggily, squinting. She crawled into the backseat with me and handed me a Mountain Dew and a cigarette, which she'd lit for me. We smoked in silence until we'd gotten down to the filters, flicked them out the open windows and sat, lost in thought.

I croaked out the words, "I hate that place."

She nodded. "Me, too." She put her arm around my shoulder. I melted into her, sobbing. She cried with me. Heartache and disappointment were poured out in wet tears and slimy snotty noses were wiped on our sleeves. When all had dried up we sat on the hood of my car watching stars and fireflies coming out. We smoked. We drank Mountain Dew. We talked some more.

When we left to go into town she turned to me and said, "We totally should have just burnt it down."

I smiled grimly in agreement. We spent the whole way back gleefully plotting the perfect arson.

The next day I hugged and kissed her before leaving to finish the drive to Iowa for college. Had I known it would be the last time in my life I'd see her, I would have done it differently. I would have clung to her longer, inhaled her perfume deeper, held her hands, memorized the details of her smile, traced the little wrinkle on the top of her nose. But I didn't know. So I simply said, "I love you, lil sis. See you soon," and drove off into my future without her.

She drove off into her future a couple weeks later, a seventeen-year-old in a stolen car with a mysterious new boyfriend. They made it all the way to what seemed like paradise to a girl who'd been born and raised in the frozen tundra of the north woods: Florida. She and I wrote back and forth and called a few times after she landed in Florida. She sounded good in her letters. She said she had a job and a place to live and hung out on the beach a lot. She said she missed me and loved me and would be back for a visit as soon as she could. She told me not to worry about her, that she was okay.

I genuinely wanted to believe her, so I did. For months I didn't worry about her, even after her letters and calls grew more infrequent, then ceased altogether. I was so busy with my studies and learning to lead a Christian life that months went by before I realized that months had gone by. I began to ask around and discovered no one had heard from her. The three a.m. phone call just after Thanksgiving break had been the last.

Now, in the spring, months after the phone call, I sat under an oak tree, unable to concentrate on my books, aching for her and fervently asking God to be close to her. I stood, absently tucked in the back of my shirt, and gathered up my books to go inside. By the time I'd reached my room, I felt it. Needles stabbed my lower back. I hurriedly dumped my books onto my dorm room floor, stood in front of the mirror on the back of my door and dropped my jeans. A red rash was welling up on my skin. I had tucked a fuzzy caterpillar into the back of my pants. It wriggled, weak and bald. I stomped it into the carpet angrily and laughed at myself, but the pain persisted.

***

Over a decade later I stood stiffly upright, hand unconsciously reaching to support my heavy stomach. I heard the deep rumble of the engine and I knew immediately it was a Harley. I paused over the birthday cake I was cutting, knife suspended in midair, and squinted toward the sound, but the road was winding and long, and I could not see it yet.

"Mommy, can I have a piece?" my daughter asked. I looked down at her and smiled. Her blue eyes were locked on the prize as I scooped it onto a little plate and handed it to her. I tucked a long strand of her blonde hair behind her ear, bent to kiss her little round cheek. She grinned at me, and tossed back an "I love you, Mommy!" as she scampered off to join her sisters. The wind pulled at her hair and I watched it blow around wildly, light and shiny corn silk.

My belly pushed against the table as I leaned forward to count my three little blonde-haired, blue-eyed girls. I rubbed my expanding baby bump in apology and returned my husband's smile as he made eye contact from across the yard.

The birthday party was a success. Almost everyone was there. My mom and dad, sisters and brother all milled around talking to each other and playing with the kids. Grandma and Grandpa sat in a swing, holding plastic coffee cups with smiley faces on them, taking it all in. I walked over to offer them some cake and heard it again, the unmistakable loud pipes of a motorcycle making its way closer. I glanced toward the sound and could make out flashes of chrome and red through the trees.

The party stopped. Everyone, even the smallest children, stood frozen, watching the bike come up the long road toward us, throwing gravel up and behind it, dust obscuring the driver. The rider parked, shut off the engine and sat looking at us behind dark sunglasses.

I stepped forward to find out who the party crasher was. The rider dismounted and shook the dust out of short, thick blonde hair. She pulled her sunglasses off and our eyes met. I stood dumbly, suddenly paralyzed. It was *her*.

Her broad smile snapped me into action. I ran awkwardly to her, supporting my heavy pregnant belly with one hand, other arm outstretched to reach her as quickly as possible. Tears streamed down my face, emotion constricted my throat. Family members yelled out her name, but it barely squeaked out of my throat—I could only speak it over and over in whispers until I was on top of her, folding her into a tight embrace. I blubbered into her neck, "Oh, God, oh God, thank you! Thank you for bringing my sister back!"

A guttural cry from somewhere in my depths escaped. I followed it, collapsed into it onto the ground with a weighty thud, abandoned to the relief and love that flooded my heart. I heard the words, "It's okay. I'm here." I felt arms wrap around me, hands rubbing my back and holding me close. "It's okay. I've got you."

I felt my face pushed against someone and reached instinctively to caress my expanding stomach, but it had somehow morphed into my own knees, which were pulled up to my chest. I rocked slightly in this fetal position. "It's okay, honey. I'm here. It's just a nightmare." I scrunched my eyes tight in response to his gentle words, attempting to ignore them, to avoid the reality. Inevitably, I sobbed into his chest long after the shadowy feelings faded, letting him comfort me. He asked quietly, "The same dream again?"

I nodded, unable to speak, unwilling to acknowledge that many years—more than ten—had passed since I'd last heard, touched, seen my sister. I wanted to stay in the dream, where she was. But no matter how hard I tried, I never could.

There have been many days where missing her was a painful stabbing bee's sting. Sometimes I expected and prepared for it the best I could, like on her birthday, Thanksgiving and Christmas. I got busier, avoiding the sting by dodging and darting from one activity to the next.

Sometimes it hit me without warning, however. At my college graduation I stood hopefully searching over the crowd for her. Sharp pangs of disappointment jabbed my heart when I realized she wasn't there; she wouldn't be coming to cheer wildly in the bleachers. At my wedding, I stood smiling in front of a full-length mirror, admiring my dress. I imagined her walking in behind me, my maid of honor coming in to fix the last stray pieces of hair. My smile faded as alone there in my dressing room I realized she wouldn't be coming in. I clenched my stomach against the punching sorrow, mustered the strength to walk down the aisle and stand at the front of the church without her, mentally covering the stings with the salve of the joy in the moment and the strength I found in the loving eyes of my groom.

Most of the time missing her was a dull ache, a fuzzy caterpillar tucked into my sub-conscience that sat in the background of my day-to-day living, a constant, unwelcome guest. I gave birth to my children, each of them achingly ironic reminders of how she looked and acted when she was little. Not being able to introduce them, except in my dreams, was yet another set of spurs jabbing me when I least expected it. No matter how many ways I tried to push it away it was still there, always under the surface, persistent barbs reminding me that she was gone. My little sister was gone.

PART TWO:

Little Sister

Chapter Five

AMERICAN GIRL

I DOUBT HE EVEN MISSES it yet. I'm flipping it over in my hands, studying it. One side's cold, smooth metal. The other's got the emblem. It was his favorite. Mine, too. I lifted it a couple days ago when he was passed out snoring on the couch. As far as dads go, he's not exactly on the ball these days. *Will he even notice I'm gone?*

Mom didn't, not for like a week. She was so busy with her new boyfriend, she didn't know I'd packed a bag and hitchhiked all the way to Dad's. I hitched a ride with this trucker dude most of the way. He was nice enough till we're about an hour away from where he was gonna drop me off. Then he starts flirting with me, says I have to "pay up" for the ride. *Aw, shit. Okay, game face.* "Sure thing, honey, but first I gotta pee real bad!" He pulls into this rest stop and I bolt outta the truck and walk the rest of the way. *Frikkin' creep.*

When Mom finally calls, she's yelling and cussing at me. Did I steal her smokes? Did I expect her to come get me? *Thanks, Mom, I love you too.* I just narrow my eyes, puff on her last nasty GPC 100 and say, "Why would I take your nasty cigarettes?" as I blow smoke into the phone. She hangs up on me. I'm just laughing into the dead receiver, "And um, no, I won't be needing a ride home, thank you very much." I'm never going back to that chaos. But I'd found a whole nother level of crazy this summer here with my dad.

There's a lot my older sister doesn't know about me, some things I done, and stuff about Mom and Dad. She is on the right track in her life now, especially since she's "found Jesus" or whatever and is going to college. She's like in a different world than me now. I don't think she gets me anymore. Like she thinks everything can just be fixed by putting your faith in God, like some magic wand or something. She doesn't get it. When I was little, I wrote on the front page of an old Bible somebody gave me, "Give me peace." What does that even feel like? I don't know. Is that even possible? I know I haven't found it yet, not the way she has, anyway. Besides I can see she's really happy and I don't wanna mess that up for her. If I can't get out of this shithole, at least I can watch her get out. Kind of gives me hope or something I guess.

I fantasized about burning down that farmhouse like a million effing times, just never had the balls to go through with it. In my daydreams, they were always in it, every single one of those bastards who'd ever hurt me, crying and begging for mercy as the fire trapped them inside. I'd yell, "Who's a big man now?" pocket my lighter and walk away. I'd be like Bruce Willis, go all Die Hard on 'em, maybe I'd whistle all nonchalantly, maybe flip 'em the finger behind my back, maybe ride away on my red custom Harley. But one thing was always the same—I never looked back.

Sitting there in my sister's car earlier today, parked in front of the little white church, I was kinda surprised when she knew exactly what I was talking about. "Let's go burn it down." Then I was worried she'd ask about why I wanted to do it, and relieved when she said we shouldn't. I don't even really know why I wanted to go there again. Maybe to see if I really could walk away.

It wasn't so bad till we got to the kitchen part of our little tour of horrors and watched that little girl walk into the bathroom. The second she opened that door, a whole chain of memories come flooding back. Him. Bloody towels. Yellow jammies. Gleaming white teeth. They hit me hard in the face like a slap. Then other ghosts come in from other rooms, from other times and places we lived. Dark demon memories flying in from all directions, scrambling my thoughts, twisting knives in my stomach. I felt that pressure in my bladder like I knew I'd pee myself, like I did in my nightmares at night, if I didn't get control again.

As we were standing there, I tried looking in my older sister's eyes for some kinda help, but hers were glued to that door, full of fear. That's right when I knew—he'd gotten to her, too. She got all wobbly, like she was going to faint or something. I got a sudden, sick feeling in the pit of my stomach—I had to shake it off, clear my mind. I remember squinting real hard and tensing up my muscles, like I just gotta barrel through this, get us the hell out of there. I reached to help her out of the house, mumbled something to the people who lived there, and took her to the car. I peeled outta the driveway and got us away as far and fast as I could. And I didn't look back once.

I let her sleep off her headache in the backseat while I sat and smoked. One of my favorite songs come on the radio and I start singing with Tom Petty real quietly so as not to wake her up. *Well she was an American girl raised on promises. She couldn't help thinkin' that there was a little more to life somewhere else. After all it was a great big world with lots of places to run to. And if she had to die tryin' she had one little promise she was gonna keep.* I made a promise to myself like that, too. I'll be free. Free of all this drama. Free of the pain.

I pull my sweatshirt sleeves up out of nervous habit. My arms are covered up and down in horizontal scars. Reminds me of all the shitty boyfriends who dumped me. Parents who broke promise after promise. The darkest night of my life is etched right there, deep in my wrist. *Jesus, I was such an idiot I couldn't even get killing myself right. Whiskey and a butcher knife. Stupid.*

I turn my arms and hands to admire the homemade ink tattoos my friends and I pushed into my skin over the years. Names, crosses, peace signs and smiley faces — all souvenirs of the pain I chose — a weird, good kind of pain. It's hard to explain, but it makes me feel tough and in control, not weak and helpless like the pain in my heart tries to make me feel.

I remember glancing back at my older sis sleeping in the backseat. Ha, she had drool plastering her hair to the side of her face. Man, I wished we were little kids together again. Riding bikes. Sledding down the biggest hills we could find. Eating Fun Dips on the swings at the park.

Hell, I wished we were teenagers again. Sneaking out of the house to find a party. Stealing cigarettes from the grocery store. Talking all night long about boys.

She was always so dang perfect, it drove me crazy. Everyone always thought she was the good kid and I was the bad one, so I got in trouble even if it was her fault. She starts the curtains on fire—Mom blames me. We both steal money from Mom's boyfriend—they blame me. I'm not saying I was innocent, but neither was she. After awhile, I just stopped arguing and let 'em all think what they wanted to. It was just like in Pretty Woman where Vivian says, "People put you down enough, you start to believe it." Edward says, "I think you are a very bright, very special woman." Then Vivian says, "The bad stuff is easier to believe. You ever notice that?" I noticed.

It wasn't any better in school either. From early elementary, teachers were always disappointed. They expected me to be like my older sister, but I'm not. She got good grades and kissed their butts. I doodled on my textbooks and got detention for cussing them out. School just wasn't my thing. Now, if somebody graded me on my out of school activities, I would have made honor roll. I laughed out loud thinking about my fake report card. Check it out: "A" in Party Hardy 101, "A" in Kicking Ass, "A" in Looking Cool on a Bike.

My sis was finally starting to come out of her sleep and sat up real slow. I could tell her head still hurt by how she was squinting against the light and rubbing at her temples. "What time is it?"

"Time for a smoke. Move over." I climbed into the

backseat next to her and handed her a cigarette and a pop. We just sat there, silent. I didn't wanna talk about what just happened or why. Neither did she. You don't talk about it, it goes away, right? That's what I thought anyways.

"So what time you heading out tomorrow?" I ask her.

"Early," she breathes out a couple of smoke rings. I watch 'em spread out and disappear in the warm air.

"You know there's colleges here, too." I knew exactly why she wanted to go far away, but it was the closest I could come to telling her I'd miss her, already missed her.

She looked hard at me, all serious. "I know. But I've been praying a lot about it, and I think God wants me to go to this school in Iowa." God, I had to look away; she had this intensity in her eyes. It was always there now, like she was looking into my soul, and I was pretty sure she wouldn't like what she saw there.

Now she was speaking that other "churchy" language she'd picked up with those other soul-searcher friends of hers who I liked to avoid. All they talked about was "God" and "His will" and "the power of prayer" and stuff like that. *Gimme a break.* They were nice people, but some of the stuff I'd done kind of put me in a different game, meaning I didn't get to play what they were playing—not with their goody-goody kind. It was weird that my older sister had become one of them.

I wasn't the only one who noticed, either. I remember one night last summer when I was getting high with some of our mutual friends. "Haven't seen your sister around anymore. She too good for us losers now that she found Jesus?" one of 'em asks all sarcastically.

"Sister Christian, man!" Everyone laughed. I just glared at the kid who said it. He was some dumb little wannabe nerd trying to fit in with us stoners. The only reason we let him hang out with us was because he always had enough weed to go around. He giggled and took a hit off the joint we were passing around. He looked like a bug in those thick wire rimmed glasses.

"I heard she's going off to some Bible college to sing Kum-By-Yah." That got more laughs, and then a few drunken singers launch into the song.

I'd had about enough. "Yeah, whatever," I muttered and stood up to leave.

I was walking right past the nerdy kid when he adds another jab, "Bet she's gonna major in missionary position." I backhanded the little shit so hard in the face his glasses flew off. He crumpled to the ground holding his cheek. I could already see a large red welt shaped just like my hand on his pasty white skin.

The room got real quiet as I walked to the door. I yelled back, "You guys better just shut the hell up about my sister. She's a better person than any of us will ever be."

Looking at her now, sitting with her in her car, playing with my stolen lighter as she's about ready to head off to her new life in college, I realize I believe the words I'd thrown back at those idiots at the party. She would be somebody and do amazing things with her life. Suddenly I have this overwhelming desire to go with her, to make something of my life, too. I get the courage to speak up, "Hey, sis, I was just thinking…"

"Yes?" She waited, I think I saw something like hope

in her eyes.

Then like a heavy window slamming down, I think about the impossibility of it—of me staying clean, me being good, me following a bunch of religious rules, me staying away from boys and bikes and rock-n-roll. Nah, that was her life, not mine. I wasn't meant to be the good girl.

"Um, I'm proud of you, you know."

I could tell I took her by surprise. "Thanks, kiddo. I love you."

I know why she doesn't say she was proud of me in return. But part of me wished she could have.

The next morning I wave and smile on the outside as she drives off—but inside I feel like the little girl who'd thrown a fit until the neighbor boys ran in and fetched me a shirt. Except this time I want somebody to bring me my big sister.

Chapter Six

LITTLE RUNAWAY

THE BEST AND WORST TWO things of my life happened on the same night, at the same party. I tried blow for the first time and I met him. I done plenty of drugs and drank and smoked pot since I was real young. Popped my share of pills and tripped on acid once or twice, but hard drugs were for the rich and famous, or at least people with money. Me and my friends may have had the desire, but we didn't have the connections. He did.

I noticed him right when he walked in the door. He stood there for a minute like he was looking for someone. *Damn. He's cute.* Early twenties, tall, with wavy shoulder length brown hair, sweet suede jacket, leather boots. I look over and his steely grey eyes lock onto mine from across the room and he smiles. He's so cute I can't help but grin back, then I get control of myself and look away, totally embarrassed. So I pretend like I'm concentrating on rolling this joint on the coffee table in front of me. When I pull it up to my lips I can feel his eyes on me. I pretend not to notice and take my slow sweet time licking the paper shut. I lay it next to the others on the table in front of me and look over at him real casual. His face is more serious now.

I can tell I'm turning him on. I hold his gaze for a minute, enjoying my power. He smiles again, walks over and asks, "Mind if I sit here?"

"Sure." I pretend not to care either way, but move over to make room for him on the couch next to me.

"Looks like you've been busy," he gestures toward the table.

I shrug, "Yeah, well, gotta keep the party going."

"You like to party, huh? I could tell when I first saw you that you're different from the other girls here. Like you know what's up, you know?" He was right, but I wasn't sure what his angle was yet, so I just shrug again. "Here, I've got something that'll make you fly. You want to really have some fun?" He doesn't wait for me to answer before he pulls out a little bag of coke. He pushes the pot over and starts setting up little lines. I watch, mesmerized. I've seen it done on TV, and I knew this was what my dad and his friends were doing in the other room after they told me to get lost. But here, with this sexy stranger sitting next to me, his leg bumping into mine, sending electricity through my body, this was already a rush. I can't wait to see what's next.

"You know what to do?"

"Of course." I don't want him to know how inexperienced I am. "You gonna do some first?"

"No, baby. I get my highs in other ways. I just wanna see you have a good time. You deserve to have some fun. I can tell you're really special." His voice is so sweet. And that smile. *He makes me feel so good. I can trust this guy.* He reaches over, grabs my hand and looks deep into my eyes. "Really special." *I'm melting.*

When he pulls his hand away, he leaves a hundred dollar bill in mine. I grin, roll it up into a tube and move closer to the table to snort my first line. Bliss. That night and every day after I'm either totally wrecked from it or chasing it. And my sexy new boyfriend has a generous, steady supply. He keeps telling me how much he loves seeing me happy. Then he's telling me he loves me, and I know it's true. And I know I'm in love with him, too. Especially after he starts talking about getting me out of the hellhole I'm living in.

I actually bring it up one day. We're lying in bed together in this motel room. His arm's around me, my head's resting on his shoulder. He pulls me close and strokes my hair with his other hand. "I love you, babe," he whispers.

I can't remember ever being this happy. I lean up and kiss his cheek. "I love you, too. I wish we could be together like this all the time."

"Me, too. If only you were just a little older, we wouldn't have to go sneaking around."

"Yeah, well, my age doesn't matter. I do what I want. I've been thinking about just leaving."

"What about school?"

"What about it? It's never been my thing. I hate it; it's a waste of time."

"What about your family?"

"What about them? My sister's gone and I'm tired of watching my siblings so Dad can get high all the time" … my voice feels a little shaky, kinda angry.

"Sorry, babe. I didn't mean to upset you." He rubs my back and pulls me closer to him. "I'll help you, if you really wanna leave."

I pull back and study his face. "You will?"

"Sure. We just need a car and we can head south. I have some friends in Florida."

I sit up now, excited at the prospect. "Florida? I've always wanted to go there! Yes! We can hang out at the beach and go to Disney World!"

He smiles. "And get high?"

"And get high! And be together every day!" I jump into him, laughing and kissing his face. *This is like a fairytale. Could this really happen?* I can feel the strength in his muscular arms as he holds me close. *Thoughts of our life together...away from here...someone who truly loves me.* He rolls me over and makes love to me again before I sneak out to go home. I'm walking on clouds, but leaving him is like agony, and I'm starting to hate it. Daydreaming about being in his arms again gets me through the moments we're separated. Now I fantasize, too, about running away with him. I'm almost too giddy with excitement to recognize it when the moment presents itself. Luckily he isn't.

Dad and I are in the middle of another big fight, which consists of him trying to tell me what to do and me throwing back in his face the fact that his life is out of control, so who was he to try to control mine. Our argument gets interrupted when his buddy comes to pick him up. He tosses me his keys, "Go get us some groceries and you need school supplies. Money's on the table." He walks out the door, yelling back, "You better not spend it on beer!" He and his friend laugh.

"Whatever!" I yell back, pissed, and stomp as loud as I

possibly can through the trailer to my room. I crank Guns
N' Roses on my boom box, smoke a joint to calm down,
and call my boyfriend. "Hey babe. So, I gotta go do some
stuff for my dad today so I won't see you until later."

His voice sounds sad on the other end. "Oh, that's too
bad. I really wanted to be with you today. I miss you."

"Well, I gotta go take his car and get groceries and
whatever. There's no food in this place and he left some
money to go get some stuff."

"You've got his car?"

"Yeah."

"Babe! This is our chance! I have enough money to get
us to Florida. Pack your stuff and come pick me up. I'll
be ready! You deserve so much better than this crap from
him. I'm gonna get you out of here."

"Really?" I look around at the filthy trailer and realize
it looks a lot like what I'd left with my mom. I thought
about how my dad is more focused on his drugs than he is
on me, just like my mom. The thing that made it hard to
leave Mom—the fact that I love my younger siblings and
would miss them—is the same reason I hesitate to leave
my dad.

I notice a Polaroid on the refrigerator door. It's my
older sister. She's posing with her suitcase and duffel bag
in front of the dorm at her college campus where Dad
dropped her off just a week ago. She's smiling, probably
because she did it. She escaped.

Screw it—I'm escaping, too. Here's my chance. "Let's
do it. I'll be there in a few." "Be ready for me."

"I am, honey. I've already got a couple lines laid out

67

for you. I love you." I slam down the phone, more excited than I've ever remembered being without drugs.

Now I can't get outta there fast enough. I race to my room and throw a few things into an old duffel bag I found in the closet. Clothes, hairbrush, some cassette tapes, a pack of smokes. I pull out an old cardboard box of my stuff from under the bed. Anything in here I need? A pile of letters from some friends and family. I grab that. Underneath is a stack of drawings and poetry I've saved over the years. On top is a sketch of a tattoo I still hoped to get one day. I designed it myself—a hand in the middle of the sun, gripping a star. I smile remembering when I showed it to my big sister and her telling me how cool she thought it was.

I put the stack on my bed and look in the box again. I see this ratty old black and red blanket lying in the bottom. I laugh out loud at the memories attached to it—coffee table forts, superhero capes, picnics under the weeping willow. I poke my finger through the burn hole my sister made in it that time she flicked her cigarette out the window of her car when we were out cruising. We didn't realize it had flown back in and landed in the backseat till we smelled the smoke. "Oh shit!" we both yell almost exactly at the same time. I jumped over the seat before it burst into flames and poured my backwash Mountain Dew on it. She had to pull over 'cause we were laughing so hard she couldn't drive.

I look back into the box and stop laughing when I see her. All of a sudden, I'm tearing up. I pull her out slowly and set her on my lap, softly stroke the matted yellow yarn hair. She has that sweet little smile on her face still, those same painted blue eyes gazing up at mine. Her frilly, flowery dress reminds me of all those times playing with my sis, escaping the chaos. Everything seemed so simple back then, even in the middle of all that craziness. I had those sweet times, those moments to hold onto, like nothing could touch those, no one could take those memories away from me. But I'm never getting those times back again either. *Get over it already. Life is shitty sometimes.*

I throw my ratty old Cabbage Patch doll back in the box, along with that blanket and the stupid stuff I wrote and drew. I don't need any of them things where I'm going. They'll just make me feel weak, or sad, or something. They're from a lifetime ago. Someone else's life. Not mine. I'm not gonna find happiness or peace in that box of babyish stuff. I'm calling the shots in my life now. I'm taking control of my own happiness—making my own peace. I got a boyfriend now who loves me and when we're together in Florida, none of this shit is gonna matter.

I kick the box under the bed, grab my bag of clothes and leave, all proud of myself for not looking back as I'm driving away in my dad's stolen car with a roll of his cash in my purse and his favorite lighter in my pocket.

I go to pick up my boyfriend, and after I get high, we head south. *Baby, we were born to run* comes on the radio and we're singing it at the top of our lungs, smoking weed, taking turns driving, and having a good old time. Pictures come into my mind of beaches and palm trees and the two of us so happy in our new life together. It's so amazing. I'm like a free bird. Anything's possible now. And I'm getting the hell out of Podunk, Minnesota.

We're about halfway there when my boyfriend asks me to pull into a rest area to take a break. "I'll be right back, gorgeous!" he says, kissing my forehead as he gets out. I lean back against the headrest and close my eyes to give 'em a break from all that driving. I must've nodded off to sleep, 'cause next thing I know, he's running this way, yelling for me to start the car, kinda panicky. As I reach down and turn the key in the ignition, he opens the passenger door and jumps in, slamming it shut and yelling at me. "Go, go, go! Get us out of here!" *Whoa dude, where's the fire,* I'm thinking. But I don't wait for an explanation. I just punch the shifter into reverse, and the car lurches backward real abrupt. He's freaking me out! He's yelling, "They're right behind me! We gotta get out of here!" I glance back and I don't see anyone chasing him, but I jam the car into drive, and we peel onto the exit ramp toward the interstate.

Once we're on the highway and he's calmed down I ask him, "What happened? Are you okay?"

"I'm fine, babe. They jumped me in the bathroom! Those bastards took all our money! I'm so sorry!"

Now I'm even more confused. "What do you mean, our money? I still have my dad's money in my purse. We can get there on that, right?"

"Shit, babe. I forgot to tell you that when you were sleeping, I took the money out to put with mine, you know for safekeeping. Dammit, it's all my fault, some kind of boyfriend I am."

"Don't say that! You're the best thing that's ever happened to me. Don't worry, we'll figure it out. Dad's got a bunch of Harley parts in the trunk. We can just pawn 'em for cash."

"Yeah, but pawn shops aren't gonna be open till morning and we really gotta get you safely to Florida before the cops come after us. I'm sure your parents have already called them."

"I wouldn't be so sure," I say. "If they've even noticed I'm gone yet, the police are probably the last people they'd send after me. I'd be more worried about what my dad and his friends will do to you if they catch up to you."

"Well, then we need money now. I have an idea. I've still got some blow stashed. Pull into this truck stop, and we'll see if we can make a trade."

I take the next exit, both of us kinda nervous about the measly quarter tank of gas showing on the fuel gauge. "Park near the trucks and shut the lights off," he says. He cups his hands over his eyes and looks into the dark cabs like he's studying 'em for a few minutes before telling me his plan. "Babe, I don't see any heat around here, so I'm gonna just go into the truck stop and ask around a little… see if we can get a couple of customers to contribute to our cause. You stay here, and if you see the cops show up, just come in after me, okay?"

"I guess, if it's the only way. Be careful. I love you!" I don't like the risk he's taking and I *seriously* don't like the idea of my supply running low, but we really need the money.

"I love you, too. Be right back!" He leans in and kisses me and then disappears into the night.

I start chewing on my thumbnails, looking around. *He's taking too long. Where the hell is he?* All kinds of crazy shit is going through my mind. *Maybe he ran off without me. Maybe he got jumped again.* I'm sitting there waiting for what seems like hours before he comes back. I can tell by the way he slumps into his seat he didn't sell anything. He just sits there and doesn't say a damn word, just sits there smoking a cigarette.

"Man, we're screwed." He looks at me and shakes his head. "I guess we need to call your family and have them come get you, huh?" He looks away, then all of a sudden he punches the glove box hard with his fist, "Damn!" Kinda scares me. When he looks back at me his eyes have tears in 'em. "I don't want to live without you, babe. We've got something so special. I just wanted to take good care of you for the rest of our lives, but look how I screwed everything up for you, for us."

I take his hand and look into his eyes. "Listen to me. I'm not going back. You're my life now. Let me go try to sell the stuff."

"It's no use. Nobody wants to buy from a stranger at a rest stop. I don't want you getting involved!"

"You don't think I can handle myself? I'm a big girl, you know!" I didn't like him telling me what I couldn't do.

"No, it's not that, babe. It's just that I don't want anything bad to happen to you. You're my world, too, you know. I don't want you to do anything you're not comfortable doing, but the truth is I've heard that girls can make a lot more money than guys in these types of places, you know, by keeping truckers company."

I sit there for a second, thinking about what he's asking me to do. I don't see any other option, so I shrug, "No

72

problem. What do I do?"

"You are so great, you know that? How'd I get so lucky to find you?" I feel proud inside to be *that* kind of girlfriend; I'm the cool chick who can handle any situation, the kind other guys say "man, you're girlfriend's so cool, dude" about. He hugs me and says, "Just go up to the cab of a truck and ask if the guy wants to party. And if anything bad goes down, I'm gonna be right here. I got your back."

"I know, don't worry, I got this."

"Hon, you know I'd never let you do this for us if it wasn't an absolute emergency. This is just business."

"I know." I quickly snort the blow he hands me, narrow my eyes, tense all the muscles in my body and step out of the car. "Be right back."

I'm a little nervous, but also feel this adrenaline rush, like I *got* this. I am gonna make him so proud of me. I knock on a few truck doors and I get invited in on the third one. My first experience with a john isn't like anything I've seen on TV. This guy is no Richard Gere and touching him makes me want to vomit. But I pretend to be confident and professional, like Julia Roberts. My boyfriend coached me on what to say, so I keep control of the situation by naming my price and pretending the guy's my boyfriend instead of a fat, pock-marked bastard who smells like onions and nacho cheese. When I step out of his truck after giving him what he wants, it's with a handful of what we need—cash. I go straight to the truck stop bathroom and wretch my guts out into the toilet. I'm holding my hair back behind me to keep it out of the puke, and I'm trying not to think about what I just did with a total stranger. *Shake it off, girl.* When

73

I come out, my boyfriend's sitting on the hood of the car waiting for me. I just give him this half-smile and wave the twenty-dollar bills at him. He runs up, hugs me around the waist and swings me around in celebration. "I'm so proud of you, babe! You did it! That's my girl!"

Between my truck stop contributions and pawning off the parts in the trunk we make it all the way to Florida. When we get to Daytona Beach, we sell the car. That's when all hell breaks loose.

Chapter Seven

FREE-FALLING

THE FIRST TIME HE HITS me, it's definitely my fault. I'm smarting off in our motel room. I come out of the bathroom after a long, cleansing shower and see him digging through my purse. He tells me I should've gotten more money for what I did in the next room for the john we met earlier in the bar. He accuses me of pocketing the rest. "Well, if you hadn't pocketed my money in the first place, I wouldn't have to do this, now would I?" Before I know what's what, he backhands me hard across the face. I land on the floor, stunned and hurt. I stay down on the floor for a few minutes not moving—partly out of shock, and partly because I want the asshole to know he really hurt me. Then this anger starts welling up in me. *I don't need this shit.* I would have walked out right then if he hadn't started crying and apologizing.

"Oh, babe, I'm so sorry. I just hate you having to do this for us. It makes me crazy to think about you with other men, you know? You belong to me. I never want to hurt you. I just...you make me feel crazy sometimes. I love you so much. I'm sorry, honey. Please, don't go. I need you so much. Don't ever leave me." He moves slowly toward me on the floor and I let him pull me into his arms, ever so slowly feeling my anger melt away as he tenderly touches my cheek where he just smacked it. "I'm so sorry. You just, you make me so crazy. I can't stand that I put you into this position for us. You're so great, you know. You're strong and I know you can handle all this. I just hate it. I'm sorry I lashed out. It won't ever happen again. I promise."

Then I'm comforting him. I hold him and tell him it's okay, that it was my fault for saying what I said to him. That yes, I'm tough and I'll be okay. That I wasn't doing anything I didn't want to. That our life together's worth it all. I loved him, I would never leave him, I was sorry for making him react so violently. That night he holds me close all night long, kissing me and whispering how much he loves me, how lucky he is to have found me, how good we are together. My body and my mouth forgive him, and we snuggle close. I know he loves me, because he says so. But inside me there's this hard little knot forming—a stubborn little part of me rising up, a little corner of my brain that's asking god-knows-who, *Is this love?* I don't understand. I stash it away for now.

In the morning I wake up to an empty motel room. A note on the coffee table next to the lines he'd set up for me says he's gone for cigarettes and he'll be right back. Hours later he appears, smelling like beer and perfume. When I ask him where he's been, he says it's none of my business; he had things to do. When I ask him if he's been with someone, he says, "Of course not. You're the only one I love. But things are a little more complicated now with you working with those other men. It's hard for me, you know."

The knot inside me turns a little harder, and I feel it physically hurt, but I hear myself say, "It's okay, hon, I know; it's just business. It's what we gotta do to survive right now." I go to hug him. He pulls away.

"Well, it's just that I have some other problems on my hands and you can't do anything about those. I'm stressed out for sure. I'm in a lot of trouble." He sits down on the bed, shakes his head sadly and folds his hands in his lap.

"What's going on?"

"Well, my dealer fronted me that coke we've been using, and he's got word out that he's looking for me, and it's time to pay up. My plan was to sell it all in Minnesota. You know, make a good profit and come back and pay him. But then I met you and plans changed. I got, well, distracted."

"And robbed!"

"Yes, and robbed. Anyways, I shouldn't have even come back here without his money. But you wanted to come here, and I got caught up in helping you, and now I've just brought you into a bigger mess. I can't even get a job to work off the debt because if he finds out I'm in town, he'll come after me. He'll come after you. You should get as far away from me as you can."

"No, we're in this together. We'll figure this out. Don't worry."

For the next couple of months, life is an almost normal routine of me earning money by meeting up with johns at different motels. As long as I have cocaine before and a hot shower and more coke after, I can almost forget about the in-between. I know I'm one of the youngest, freshest girls out there hustling, and business is good. How it works is, I catch the john's eye, like on the beach, on the street, in a store—wherever. He asks if I wanna party. I ask if he's a cop. He says no and we go to a room. Simple. Then, first thing, I excuse myself to the bathroom to, you know, "freshen up." I do some drugs, squinch my eyes, tighten every muscle in my body, psych myself up, and go get the job done. Even when the guy's rough—or worse, sayin' he's sorry—I don't react any different. Street smart, cocky, tough. That's how I keep control of the situation. It's how I keep control of myself.

The rest of the time we're hanging out on the beach, eating out, acting like a normal couple in love. Sometimes when I feel a little nostalgic, I write or call my sister. On Thanksgiving Day we're at McDonalds's and I'm eating a burger, pretending it's filling me up, and wishing I'm home with her, the two of us gorging ourselves in our annual eating contest. I call her a couple of days later and tell her how happy I am in Florida. I have a job and am thinking about going back to school. I tell her about the beach and how great my boyfriend is. I tell her maybe I'll be home to visit for Christmas. I tell her one lie after another. I tell her what she wants to hear.

It's when I lay in bed at night that the loneliness hits me across my heart, as sure and as hard as my boyfriend's hand hit me across the face that day. Jesus, I miss my big sister. I just wanna tell her what's really going on in my life. I wanna ask her for help, to come rescue me. But I can't. She's living her life, making it good. She's genuinely happy.

I don't want to ruin that for her.

In the darkness, lying next to him, I feel how pointless the life I'm living is. Any money I bring in, I snort away, or we spend it on crappy motels, drinking, eating or buying junk. Every friggin' time we get a little bit saved up, something happens. We gotta bribe a motel manager not to turn us in. Somebody recognizes my boyfriend, and he has to pay up so the dealer won't get word he's in town. A pimp accuses us of being in his territory, and we have to pay him off not to break my boyfriend's legs. We know a couple of cops who'll look the other way for the right price. It's stressful and expensive, living this way. I'm exhausted all the time—always looking over my shoulder, wondering when the bottom's gonna drop out. I'm getting tired of having all the pressure on me to make all the money, but I just don't see any way out.

At least we're together. I look over at him and snuggle up closer, thankful for his warm body next to mine. I like how his brown wavy curls fall on his face and the pillow. I drift off to sleep, looking forward to the lines I know he'll have set up for me in the morning. My next high and his love for me keep me going from one god-awful day to the next.

When he cuts me off of both, things really get bad. I awake to, "It's gone, babe. I can't get any more without going to my contacts and they can't know I'm in town, remember?" I am flipping out. My anger's boiling up, I mean I am HOT angry, like a raging maniac, and I throw a Mountain Dew can at him because that's all I can find, and it's a good thing there isn't a gun lying around. Anger comes, and then panic... *I can't do what I do with those disgusting men without the drugs.*

I turn to him, white-hot furious, and spit the words, "I'm not going to keep making money for you to piss away on booze and other women! I'm done!" This time his fist is closed when it makes contact with my stomach. I double over in pain, and watch him storm out. I'm so pissed I'd kill him for sure if I could catch my breath.

Two days go by, and I don't see him. I go from being really depressed to really angry to practically manic. I'm really on the edge here. I want drugs. I feel like I got the flu. I sleep a lot, but my dreams are full of corpses. I can even smell the death in my dreams. I bum some smokes off other motel guests, and I fly into a rage when I can't find my lighter. I'm really losing it. I tear the room apart—pull out drawers, flip over the mattress, smash a lamp against the wall. Where is it? I crumple onto the floor in a pathetic little pile and pound my fists weakly into the carpet. *Where is he?*

I wanna go home. I want my sister, my mom and dad. I curl up into a ball and cry, deep choking sobs. I have nothing—no money, no car, no way to light my damn cigarette. I'm so tired. My tear soaked, snot-matted face presses into the filthy carpet. I imagine myself melting right into the old pizza, mud, and body fluid stains, just disappearing right into the carpet. People would come in and walk right over me and not know I was there—just another stain on the floor. If I could have done so just by willing it, I would have. I lay there wishing it were that easy and daydreaming about my options. I could use the razor in the bathroom. I could tie a sheet around my neck and hang it over the ceiling rafters. I could push a pen into the light socket. I could take every pill I could find. But I just really don't have the energy to do anything more than lie here and think about possible ways to end it all. I wish someone would do it for me. I fall back asleep.

When I wake up, it's dark in the room. I'm panicky at first, not sure where I am. I sit up and squint; my eyes feel all puffy and swollen. I try to get my bearings. A motel streetlight pushes random rays through a hole in the thick, musty curtains and I sit, blinking in surprise. There on the floor lay a matchbook, near an overturned bedside table. Its metallic cover glints brightly, catching my eye. *Where were you when I needed you before?* I snatch it up, grab my broken cigarette and light it there in the dark room. I smoke it down like a fiend, then stand shakily and pocket my find. I can think of only one way out of this lonely mess, and if I'm gonna do it, I better do it now before I lose my nerve or the will to act on it.

Shit, I see on the clock that it's four a.m. But I can't wait; I have to call her right away. It's gotta be now or never. I dial her number and wait for someone in the dorm to pick up. I'm surprised when she answers, "Hello?"

"Hey, it's me." I wanna cry the minute I hear my big sister's voice, but I try to keep mine normal so I don't scare her and make her think something's up. She keeps asking me if I'm okay and I tell her I am. Lies lies lies—I try not to cry, try to act happy like her, make small talk, she jokes, I laugh. She sounds so…good.

Talking to her makes me feel even dirtier than I had

before. I look around at my filthy motel-trash life. It's all shit. I'm ready to be done with it. "Yeah, I'm okay, I promise. I love you, too. Talk to you soon, bye."

I go to the bathroom and grab the razor. I feel like I'm in a daze now or a trance or something. Like a ghost. That's it, like I'm already gone. All I have to do now is go through the steps. I sit on the edge of the tub, dig out the blade from the plastic handle with a pen and hold it, turning it over and over in my hands. I run it loosely on my leg first, just above my shorts line. Red instantly dots the small, superficial cut. Numbly I cut deeper, longer on my thigh. I feel nothing as I watch blood run down my leg in narrow trickles. It tickles my foot as it pools on the floor, warm and sticky. I just watch. I lay my arm across my lap and grip the razor in my other hand hard enough to draw blood on my finger. "I'm sorry, God. I just can't do this anymore. I hope you can forgive me," the prayer barely makes it out. I narrow my eyes, clench my teeth, tense every muscle in my body and angrily sweep my arm in a vicious circle to jab the blade into my wrist and sever my arteries, sever my limb, sever my life from the pain forever.

He catches my arm mid arc in his strong grip. "What are you doing? Oh no! I knew I shouldn't have left you here alone! Oh God! Come here, babe! Let me hold you! It's okay now, I'm here! I got you!" I'm being carried into the bedroom, and he sits me in a chair, and I half-see out of blurry eyes he's setting up a line of coke for me. He's doing something over by the bed now, straightening the blankets I think, and then he carries me gently to it, tucks me in and lies down next to me. He's stroking my hair like when we first met, whispering apologies and tender words. I feel so weak and small. I let him comfort me. I disappear into his love, allowing contentment to swallow me up as I surrender to the drugs and his gentle touches and tone.

I never mention his sucker punch and he never mentions my suicide attempt. It's like they never happened, but it's also like they did, if that makes sense—things were the same, but would somehow never be the same. Our life was looking up again—no reason to bring up the past. He was back, he had drugs, he made promises to take care of me, and we start plannin' our happily ever after again.

A few days later, we're lying lazily in bed. He smiles at me and says, "I have great news, babe. I went to my supplier and told him everything. How the Minnesota market is a really solid lead, how hard we've been working to get the money we owe him, but how things keep falling through. He said we could work directly with him to pay off our debt and that he'd protect us. He wants me to firm up my northern connections. You wanted to go back to Minnesota for Christmas, right?"

"Really? Wow! Are you serious? Yes! Let's do it!" I hug him, like crazy-excited.

"He wants to meet you, babe. I told him all about you, how beautiful and loyal and hardworking you are. So many women here are weak, you know. What you've been through would break them. But you are strong and smart and beautiful, and..." he laughed wildly, "I already said that, didn't I? Beautiful! Beautiful! Beautiful! And I love you so much!"

That makes me giggle, I enjoy his affection. "Okay,

cool. When do I meet him?"

"How about tomorrow? And afterwards I'm going to take you to Disney World!"

"Deal! Oh, babe, you really are the best thing that's ever happened to me! I love you so much!"

The next morning I wake up early, super excited. I drop a letter in the mail for my big sis, scarf down some donuts and juice in the motel lobby, and bring some back to the room for my boyfriend, who is still sleeping. I don't wanna wake him, so I go outside and sit on the bench in front of our room to smoke. I feel around in my pockets for a lighter, but come up with the book of matches I found in my room that awful night instead. I scratch the head of the last match against the sandpaper strip and watch it flare up. I just stare, frozen for a second as the flame burns yellow, red and blue on the end of the cardboard. Light.

I push it against the end of my cigarette, inhale deep to ignite the paper and tobacco, then casually watch the flame walk up the rest of the match stick and burn itself out in a puff of smoke near my finger and thumb. I think about how darkness is blindness, numbness, emptiness and sometimes terror, like when I woke up alone in my motel room. Light can be so warm and comforting, like the sun at the beach, but it can also be harsh and glaring when it illuminates the shit that's better off left in the dark. Light is harder to grasp and it burns. It hurts to feel and see the things that really are there, which is much worse than just the fear of what might be.

I flip the matchbook over and read, "Are you in trouble? We can help. Call the Free Hotline at 1-800-RUNAWAY."

I puff slowly on my cigarette, thinking about all the poor girls who've run away from home and ended up in much worse situations than me. They didn't have a boyfriend like mine to watch out for them. They didn't have the street smarts and strength I did to do what needed to be done to survive out here on my own as a teenage girl. I grind my cigarette butt into the arm of the black metal bench, flick the empty matchbook into the parking lot and walk into the room to see my boyfriend lining up my morning high. *Life is pretty good,* I think. *No, I don't need any help.*

What a difference a few hours can make.

Chapter Eight

PARADISE CITY

I NEVER MAKE IT TO Disney World, in case you hadn't already guessed, but I sure did end up on a wild ride over the next couple of months. We go to meet my boyfriend's drug supplier one day. He's this greasy haired guy, older than us, with bleached white teeth and a big laugh. He looks me up and down, glances at my boyfriend and says, "She's definitely got potential." I'm not sure what that means, but it's the first time I've ever heard it, and somewhere deep down, I know he's right.

My boyfriend tells me he has a meeting with our host, hugs me quick and whispers in my ear, "Remember, it's just business, babe." I watch the two of them walk into an office, then decide to have a look around the place.

It's really nice, practically a mansion. There's lots of people partying in pretty much every room. He told me to make myself at home, so I do. There's food and drinks and drugs everywhere. People are dressed really nice, with lots of fancy jewelry on the women. Classy set-up. Couples are pairing up and heading into different bedrooms. I feel like a kid in a candy store. I find someone with some coke, and after I do a few lines, I look around for my boyfriend, but I can't find him anywhere. I walk outside and our host finds me. "He's gone."

"What do you mean? Like he ran to the store?"

"No, dear. He's left you. He brought you here to pay off his debt. Why don't you stay with me for a little while, see what I do and become part of the business?" He kinda waves toward the house. "I can offer you so much. I take good care of my girls. They have a plentiful supply of whatever drugs their little hearts desire, nice clothes, good food and jewelry. All you'd have to do is take care of business when I needed you. Someone as young and hot as you can make loads of dough here. You'll pay off your debt in no time."

"What the hell? No, I'm gonna go find him. This is crazy. He wouldn't just leave me like this."

"Here, he left you this note."

He hands me a scrap of paper with the words "It's over between us. It's just business, babe. Don't come after me" scrawled across it in his familiar handwriting. Now I'm pissed. I crumple the paper and throw it on the driveway.

"Whatever, I'm outta here!"

"Suit yourself, it's your choice. But you've met me and know where I live and some might call me paranoid, but I can't just let you leave and go tell the cops all about me, now can I?"

"I'm not a narc! I wouldn't tell anyone anything! I just gotta go find him."

"You won't find him. I've already sent him back out. He's half-way to Minnesota by now to find new business for me."

"He was going to take me with him!"

"No, honey, he wasn't. He was always going to bring you to me. He never truly cared about you, sweetie. He told you what you wanted to hear so that he could use you. He had a substantial debt to me, as you know—one that you helped increase. He has brought you to me as payment. You can work here for me for a while, pay off your debt, and then you will be free to go. I promise."

"No thanks, mister. I can get home on my own," I say, but I wonder if it's true.

"Of course. Just know that I cannot guarantee your safety out there. A lot of really bad things happen to young runaway girls down here. They get hurt. They disappear. They are found washed up on the beach. I would hate for that to happen to you. Just stay here with me for a little while, work off the debt, and I will make sure you get home to Minnesota safely. I promise."

He said the magic word, Minnesota. *Hmm...* I take a long drag from my cigarette... *How bad could working for him be? Can't be any worse than being with a guy who can't get a job, smacks me around, runs out of snow, and comes home smelling like perfume. Oh, and freaking* leaves *me! Right? Well, what choice do I have in the matter, really?* "Alright, I'll stay, but just for a little while." To anyone watching I looked confident and in control, like I want to be there. Inside I'm completely terrified. I feel trapped, but I vow to find my way out as soon as possible. I'll survive, get out of this mess, and then laugh about it later. But first I'll play along for a while.

"That's a good girl. It's just business. Remember that

and you'll get along well in life down here."

"Sure, whatever you say. It's just business," I echo as I follow him back inside the dark, smoky house. Everybody's drinking and doing drugs. Guys are pairing up with girls and moving like ghosts in and out of the bedrooms that lined the hallways. I think I know what his "business" is, but too soon it's my turn. The host walks me to a door, swings it open and tells me to go in and get undressed.

"Um, no. I don't think so. I have a say in how I work."

He just laughs this kind of condescending laugh, pushes me in and shuts the door. The latch on the outside closes with a loud click, locking me inside. My big sister's words about the rusty cage from our childhood echo in my mind, "You can't escape from everything, you know. Some things are too strong for you." I look around, terrified, hating that she was right.

The room has a large red and black velvet-covered poster bed in the middle of it, complete with mirrors on the ceiling and walls. *Jesus.* I stand there, wondering exactly what kind of mess I've gotten myself into and wishing I was high, when a different door opens and four burly college guys come in. "So, this is the girl who likes it rough, huh?"

When I protest, they think it's part of my act, and for the next few hours, they each take turns having their way with me. Deep inside me the knot clenches tighter and goes numb. I'm somewhere, anywhere, nowhere, just not here. When they're done, I lie naked, exhausted and broken in the middle of the bed where I'm still tied. I can't utter a sound. One of the guys walks over to a cabinet on the other side of the room and pops out a VHS tape. "This'll be a fine souvenir, boys!"

Humiliated, I realize that someone has videotaped the entire thing. They leave, laughing and high-fiving. Closing my eyes, I hope never to wake up again. When I do, it is to a breakfast of pancakes and cocaine. My host unties me gently. "I'm sorry they were so rough with you. That's not the way I'd hoped your first time would go." The gracious bastard pulls a blanket over me, helps me sit up and serves me my food on a tray in my bed. "You did very well, my dear. Let me tell you an important business secret. The more pleased my customers are, the better it is for you. You will have your debt paid off to me in no time!"

My body betrays me then, and I begin to cry. He pulls me into some kind of sick, fatherly hug. "There, there, dear. Your boyfriend was right, you know. You are a very strong one. I have no doubt that you will be just fine. You can make a lot of money in this business, you know. You could be a real professional!" He strokes my hair, leans close to my ear and whispers, "I'm going to take good care of you. It won't ever be as bad as last night. I promise."

He did keep that part of his promise—that was the first and last time I didn't get good and loaded before a "taping." I was becoming a master at playing the game. I'd squinch, tighten my muscles, and go through the door to deal with whatever was behind it with my brave face on. Thanks to the drugs, most of the time I was in a mist, floating in and out of rooms like the other girls. Men of all ages and types passed me around for sex, and I reminded myself again and again that it was just business. I worked all the time and even though I had no idea how much I owed, or how much he was making off me, I really thought my host would come in one morning and tell me I was done. Or that my boyfriend would walk in and tell me he paid off our debt and I was free to go. It never occurred to me that the cocaine I was using to cope with my "work" was being charged to my account.

He sets me straight one day a few weeks later, "Listen, honey. You're doing a real good job here and I don't mind sharing my supply with you—I really don't. But you're costing me more than you're bringing in. You're going to have to increase productivity, you understand?"

After that I go from a few tapings a day to a dozen. I'm barely sleeping or eating. I'm so physically and emotionally worn out from pretending to enjoy the abuse of anyone who enters my room that I can't seem to get enough junk to keep me going, and I shut down. I just effing shut down. I lay there staring into space like a freakin' zombie—can't even get up, like catatonic. At some point—I don't know when—my host comes in to check on me. "You poor dear, you're suffering from exhaustion, I think. You Minnesotan girls with your strong work ethic—you've about worked yourself to an early grave, you silly thing." I float in and out of consciousness.

I can hear bits of conversation with an unfamiliar female voice. "Let me take her. I can help her get back on her feet."

"I don't want her on her feet." Laughter. I sleep some more, and deeply.

"She's so young...has so much to offer."

"Well, not to me. She's a liability. Costs too much to

keep her high enough to work!" My host sounds angry.

The woman again, "I'll take care of her. I'll get her cleaned up." I drift in and out again, maybe for hours, or it could have been days. I don't know how long I'm lying there.

When I wake up again, I'm in a clean, soft bed, tucked into a comfy quilt. The room is bright; sunlight's streaming in through an open window, practically blinding me, but it feels good. There's a woman sitting in a chair next to my bed. She's wearing black leather pants and a stretchy brown velvet shirt. Her hair is bleached blonde, currently in rollers. "Hi, sugar." She smiles. I recognize her voice and attempt a smile back. "I'm here to help you."

"I know," I whisper gratefully.

For the next week, all I do is rest. She brings me some clean clothes, food and cigarettes. *Who is this lady? Some kind of good Samaritan? No one's ever treated me this way. Like she doesn't want anything back. Maybe I can trust her.* Before long I start letting my guard down and we become friends. She asks me all about where I grew up and how I got to Florida. She tells me she's never had a daughter of her own, but when she saw me in the "Taping House," she knew right away she wanted to help me. She says I can live with her and go back to school. "I think you should call your family and tell them you're okay." I do, and for the first time in a long time, it was actually the truth.

My new friend and I get real close, real quick. She's like a mom and a best friend rolled into one. We go shopping, do our nails, play cards and watch TV. She leaves sometimes, either at night or random times of the day, for like a few hours. She'll get a phone call, then tell me she'll be right back—"Time to make the donuts!" I figure she's maybe cleaning houses, or at worst, selling pot. I know she isn't an angel, same as me. She's just a good person who likes to have some fun once in a while. We drink and smoke pot together, *but she's too nice to be doing anything too shady*, I think.

When she finds out I come from a biker family she gets excited, "You know about Bike Week, right? I make a ton of money!"

"Making donuts, I suppose?" *Ha ha.*

She smiles, "No, not making donuts, but I don't want you getting involved. You need to focus on getting back into school. You're young and you have your whole life ahead of you to learn how to make the big money."

I don't like her telling me I'm too young. "I hate school. What's the point if I can make money without it?"

"Well, no offense, but I'm just not sure you're ready. You have a family who still cares about you…"

"Correction—I have an older sister who still cares about me. Nobody else gives a shit."

"Well, I just mean that you still have a chance to go home, to do things the right way. For me, there's no turning back; I've been at this so long. But you still get to decide."

"Decide what? I don't even know what you're talking about!"

"I'm not sure that you're ready—that you're strong enough to bring in yet. I'd have to test you."

"Like I said, I hate school, especially tests!" I joke. She doesn't even laugh. "Okay, what's the test?"

"We about lost you at the Taping House."

"Yeah, well, I got sick. That happens. I did the work. I never got any money. That sucked."

"You did work really hard. Hard enough to have paid off your debt. That's why he let me take you home with me. No, the business opportunity I have is a bit more involved than what you were doing there, and you would actually be paid. A lot." Now I'm listening real hard. "But I'm not ready to bring you in yet. I have to know it's the right thing for you. You're kind of like my daughter now, you know."

She hugs me. "So, speaking of donuts, you want to get something to eat?"

I hug her back. "Sure, but this time it's on you." We laugh.

I drop the subject but watch her closer over the next week or so. I start to see a pattern. When she comes home from her mysterious outings, she always does two things: carries a white business envelope into her room first thing, then takes a long, hot shower. She keeps her room locked when she isn't home, so I can't snoop around. One day when she's still in the bathroom, I seize the moment and slip in real quietly. I see a small safe in the corner of her room. She left it open, and there's a stack of ten or so envelopes. I can hear the water still goin' strong in the bathroom, so I creep over and real quietly lift the top one. *Crap. Sealed.* I grab one from the bottom of the pile and take it to my room quickly. I hide it under my mattress and go back to my solitaire card game on the coffee table until she comes out.

The first chance I have to examine it comes the next day.

95

As soon as I hear her drive away, I pull out the envelope and sit on my bed to open it, real carefully. I'm laughing to myself because the way I slowly push a butter knife under the fold reminds me of how my sister and I used to steal cigarettes from our mom. We'd open the cardboard carton, pull out a pack of cigarettes, slit the fold at the bottom of the pack and pull out the two cigarettes from the middle so the package wouldn't lose its shape. We'd glue it all back together when we were done and no one had a clue.

I look into the envelope, "Holy! What?" *Jesus, a stack of hundred dollar bills.* I pull 'em out and fan myself with 'em, "Why yes, I do love donuts." Not only that, I count 'em, smell 'em, trace the numbers on 'em, and flip 'em through my thumbs. What lovely money! I think about the other stacks in the safe, and suddenly I'm daydreaming about what I'd do with that much cash. I could go home. I could help my sister pay for college. I could get a sweet red Harley and ride off to wherever I wanna go.

No, not like this. Things would not go down like this. I put the money back into the envelope, reseal it and stick it back under my mattress. I might have stolen some things, sometimes, but I'm no thief. This woman's really trying to help me, and I'm not about to go taking her money. Not without trying to get her to let me into the business. She's onto something big, and I want in. Even though I know it's something shady, doing business with her feels a little more legit than outright robbing the woman. And if she doesn't let me in, I know where I can find a personal loan if I need it.

When she gets home later that day, she goes to do

her regular routine. I wait until I hear her step into the shower, then I go in her room and crouch down and put the envelope back into her safe. I stand and turn around to leave, but there she is, standing in the doorway of her bathroom, fully clothed! *Busted!* I tense, expecting her to come at me for going into her room and getting into her stuff. Nope. She just smiles and walks over to me, holding her arms out for a hug. "I am so proud of you! You passed my test! I knew you would!"

She welcomes me into her arms and her business. Basically, she's running a prostitution ring with a twist. She finds marks at high end tourist hotels, middle or high class businessmen who are lonely or just think that getting laid is a standard business trip perk. She always makes them pay upfront, keeps track of where they set down their wallet, and gives them whatever their little heart desires. Once the john is serviced and kicking back, relaxing, she grabs his wallet and snags his ID and credit cards. Now this is where the real money comes in, because she has a contact who pays big for credit cards, IDs and any personal info he can turn around and sell on the black market. She leaves the poor sap in the hotel room, too humiliated to report the theft, because then everyone would know he's been with a prostitute. He reports it lost, I guess, eventually, but the damage is already done by then.

It all sounds kind of Hollywood to me—exciting and, better yet, lucrative! Once I learn the ropes, I can't wait to start. She gets a call the next day, and I follow her into the hotel. She passes an envelope to the doorman on the way in, and it seems like it's remotely connected to his neck because his head instantly turns the other way as we walk in.

She tells me to hold out my hand and puts a little baggie in it. "You'll want this before, dear."

We lounge around the lobby for a few minutes until the mark (who'd requested company) makes eye contact with me. He smiles and walks over. "This her?" he asks my friend without taking his eyes off me.

"Yep. Sweet sixteen, just like I told you." This seems to excite the guy. I'm actually seventeen, but I know not to correct her. It's all part of the game for him and probably means more cash up front. "This is her first time, so be nice. And I'll be waiting right down here. You have an hour."

He is so eager. He grabs my hand and walks me to the elevator. Then I excuse myself to the bathroom, snort some white powder out of the baggie, go into game mode, and do everything the way she taught me. Afterwards I meet her in the lobby, feeling pretty good. "Everything alright?" she says. I pat my pocket, where his wallet's contents are bulging, and she smiles proudly at me.

She drops me off at home so I can clean up and goes to meet her contact. When she gets back, she lets me count the money and gives me half. I feel something I've never felt before in my life: rich.

Chapter Nine

HOME SWEET HOME

I'M STARTING TO USE MORE cocaine again, which is how I stomach what I do to make money—AND why I spend it as fast as I make it. I make some friends who like to party as much as I do. I think I may be too generous with my supply because pretty soon I owe my friend money. I think she would have cut me off, except she's getting half my income for doing pretty much nothing. She starts getting on my case more, nitpicking about my room not being clean and hinting about how expensive it is to feed and house me. Finally she tells me to my face that if I don't clean up my act, our business arrangement is over.

I start thinking about striking out on my own. I don't have the contacts for the identity theft stuff, but the other part I could do, as long as I can stay high enough. She talks all the time about Bike Week and how much money we'd make. There'd be a ton of bikers looking for a good time who'd want to have some company. She points out my tattoos and Harley t-shirt and tells me, "They'll like you— you're one of them!" I laugh with her, but in my mind that becomes the target date for me to make a break for it and get out on my own, like I always do when people start getting on my case. I know I can snag her little safe for startup costs. I figure the money in there is mostly mine anyways. I'm the one doing all the dirty work.

I speed up my plans when she tells me she's gonna handle my half of the money, too. I act like I'm okay with it and wait till she leaves. I already have my bag packed. I pry the lock on her bedroom door open and go in to get the safe. *Damn, I'm brilliant.* I stuff it down deep into my bag, grab a bag of weed off her dresser and leave as quick as I can.

I'm polite, so I scribble a note on a napkin I find in the kitchen: *Thanks for everything. Gone to join the circus!* We used to joke around about that. She told me that if my family ever started asking her questions about me, she'd probably just tell them I'd joined the circus. We laughed a lot about that one, especially since Ringling Brothers was about as far away from the ID scam as Disney World was from the Taping House. I frown now and walk out the door, refusing to think about how far away and alone I am from my sister, and from God, wherever he is.

I use the last cash I have for a motel room and set my heavy bag down on the bed. This is gonna be it—my fresh start! No one can tell me what to do from here on in! I'd thought ahead and picked up a hammer and pry bar at a hardware store I passed. I dig the safe out now and shove the heavy metal bar into the side with the combination. A couple of hard hits later and the lock gives way. I'm laughing now… this seems almost too easy.

When I open it, my heart sinks. Sitting there on the bottom of the safe is only one thin envelope. *The f---!* I pick it up and turn it over. There's my name on the front. I'm pissed, crying and raging now, and I tear it open to read the note inside: *Nice try, you ungrateful little bitch. You're on your own now.* It was written in dark black marker on two sides of a dollar bill.

I shrug and start to roll a joint. *Great. Whatever. I'll be fine.* I just need to get to Bike Week. Of course, I'll have to find my own dealer as soon as I get some cash, but I'll get through this. I'll smoke a quick one, then climb under the blankets and let the withdrawals run their course. *I can do this.* I grit my teeth and resign myself for the hell that's gonna be the next few days. I start feeling my pockets for my lighter, but of course, it fell out somewhere on my long walk or else I left it sitting somewhere after lighting up my smoke. *No problem,* I think, *there's probably a book of matches or something lying around the motel room.* I open the nearest bedside drawer first.

It's been so long since I've seen one that it sorta took me by surprise. I carefully pull out the hardbound book and set it on my lap. It feels solid, almost comforting in a way. Into my mind come flashes of memories now flooding in fast. There's the sweet little old Sunday school teacher who gave me hers 'cause I told her I didn't have one. I doodled poems, scribbled names of boys I loved, and wrote things I believed about God and Jesus on page after page after page.

I remember the night when I went to the book, searching, hoping for a magical fix to the mess my heart was. It was just before I left my mom's the last time that I wrote my prayer, three words, across the first page inside the cover: *Give me peace.*

Now as I lay in bed thinking about those words, tracing the letters on the cover of the book with my finger, I think about peace. I try to remember feeling it, or something like it—try to find some sense of having it at times in my life. I felt comfort when I was snuggled in bed close to my big sister. I felt safe when I was with my grandma, or with people from the little church we used to go to. *Wasn't that peace?* I felt the quiet and awe of the Northern Lights. The call of a loon echoing across the water. The whisper of the wind through the pines. But I'm not sure I know now if I have ever truly known what peace is. Maybe it's a combination of all these things. I was certain of only one thing—that I wouldn't find it here.

I wonder if it's still possible for me to go home after all that's happened. Everybody is still probably mad at me, for stealing from 'em, lying to 'em, and leaving 'em. You name it, I did it all. Holy crap. I can't go back to church, that's for sure. I didn't belong there before...how could I go there now after the things I done and the choices I made?

God has to be really disappointed in me, too. I keep doing the wrong thing, even when I know what the right thing is. Like I know suicide is wrong, yet I tried that more than once. I know drugs are wrong, but I can't seem to stay away from them. I want to feel the way they make me feel—happy. I know having sex with guys is wrong, and I'm darn sure doing it for money is wrong, and of course I stole from lots of people, too. I can't think of even one of the Ten Commandments I haven't at least attempted to break.

"I bet I know what He'd say to me if He were here in this room with me right now. He'd tell me I gotta change my ways. I gotta get straightened up and fly right." I start speaking right to the Bible. "Well, I want to, I really do. I really am sorry for how I'm messing up my life." Suddenly I'm talking to God, "I remember you, God, from when I was little. I remember the verses we learned together, my big sister and I. I remember the promises in them, and I don't claim to deserve a single one of them. But I just want to ask you again for peace."

Somehow, despite an unsmoked joint waiting for me at my bedside stand, despite my body going into cocaine withdrawal, despite the fact that I'm penniless in a town that has so far just used and abused me, I fall asleep. And I dream the most wonderful dream about a place I've never been to, a huge expanse of clouds with soft colors and a beautiful, ornate white bench sitting on one side. A smiling, shining Light sits there and beckons me to join Him on the bench. I want to run to Him, because I know His arms will hold me in peace and love and joy. I want to melt into them and never be released. But just as I'm about to reach the bench, the dream fades and I wake up, thinking that maybe I'd just been given a glimpse of peace.

Disappointed to find myself back in reality, I go to the motel lobby to find someone with a lighter. When I ask him for a light, the guy behind the counter hands me a book of matches. That familiar silver cardboard. I stare at it, turn it over thoughtfully in my hands, knowing full well what I'd find written on the back: 1-800-RUNAWAY. I realize right then that this is who I am— a runaway, a junkie, a homeless girl who doesn't belong here alone. Then the decision blooms on me like a sunrise—it's time to go home. *Yeah, I can go home. Home.* Bike Week was starting—maybe I could ride home with some cute guy on a sweet motorcycle. Or maybe I could scrounge up enough money for a bus ticket home.

I go back to my motel room and think about it, trying to formulate a plan. I have a couple relatives who sent me money over the past months, which I partied away. I had even called up my best childhood friend and told her and her mom that I was trying to escape from a boyfriend who was trying to sell me for drugs. God, I felt terrible afterward and decided I wasn't gonna con anybody I loved out of money ever again. I couldn't admit to anyone that I'd blown most of the money they sent up my nose. A couple others had offered to send me a one way ticket home. That wasn't what I'd wanted at the time, but I do now. I lost my piece of notebook paper with everybody's phone numbers on it and now I can't remember anybody's number anymore, anyway. There is no one back home left to call.

So I punch in the number: 1-800-786-2929. A kind, motherly voice answers, and before I can stop myself, I'm crying, the grief and loneliness and pain coming in waves now. I'm gasping for breath, and between sobs, I'm telling her my story, and asking her if she can help me get home. I'm crying like a little baby but I don't care anymore. I can hear myself blubbering, "I want to go home! I just want to go home!"

"It's okay, dear. We'll help you get home. That's what

we're here for. Let me come pick you up, and we can help you with the next steps."

Somehow I am coherent enough to tell her where I am, and I wait outside until a blue sedan pulls up. A car door opens and middle aged woman who looks like she could be anyone's mom steps out smiling, and extends her hand to me. "Good to meet you, dear. Now, let's go get you something to eat, shall we?"

I'm wary, but I follow her to her car, wondering what her angle is. I know all about people who "will take good care of me." But the lure of a real meal is too much for me to resist. I get in and sit down, holding my duffel bag close in my lap, and push myself hard against the inside of the passenger door as we drive off, ready to bail out if I have to.

She takes me to a buffet where I eat like I haven't in months. I'm piling up the rolls and tenderloins and mashed potatoes and she's making small talk while I stuff my face. She asks me where I'm from, if I have family there, and what grade I should be in school. When she tries to pry about how I got down to Florida, or what I've gotten involved in, I just shrug or lie. I don't know if she's with the cops, or maybe she's even connected to the shady characters I got hooked up with. There's gotta be something in it for her to be helping a perfect stranger, and a mess like me at that. Until I figure her out I decide to just keep cool.

She says there's a house she can take me to, somewhere I can get back on my feet with other girls who are coming off the streets, too. I tell her thanks, but no thanks. I just wanna go home.

She's not letting up. She tells me there's a church that sponsors the house, and that people are really nice there, and that it's a good place to get clean and rest. I tell her no, I'm not interested; I have a sister who's part of a church and they'll help me out.

Then she's telling me she's concerned about my future and whether I'd make it all the way home safely—but if that's what I really want, she'll help me get a bus ticket home. "Really?" I ask. "Why would you do that for me? You don't even know me."

"Because I was once in your shoes, and if it weren't for the grace and mercy of God, I wouldn't have survived the streets." She goes into more of her story, and I'm connecting with a lot of it. There's lots of Jesus talk mixed in—stuff I don't understand—but her eyes are shining and happy and kind, like my sister's. When she pulls up in front of the bus station, I know she's serious.

She buys me a ticket to Minnesota. Then she asks me if she can pray with me and I let her. She tells me she wants to hug me and I let her. She says if I change my mind or need any more help to call her. She walks outta the bus terminal to go rescue some other hard-headed girls like me and I let her. I am so excited to go home!

My bus doesn't leave for another half hour, so I stuff my ticket into my duffel bag and go have a smoke outside. I'm sitting against the wall on my bag when I hear this loud, thundering line of Harleys drive past. I stand up and walk closer to the road to watch 'em rumble by. My heart's beating real fast, and I probably have this big stupid grin on my face. Forget Bike Week, there's plenty of motorcycles where I come from. If Dad forgives me, which I know he will, because like he always says, "The apple don't fall too far from the tree," he and I can work on his old bike together, like we used to. And if Mom forgives me, which I know she will, because she understands me like no one else does, then she and I can hang out and play video games or whatever together, like we used to. And if my sister can forgive me, which I know she will because she's trying to do all the stuff Jesus taught, then maybe she and I can go to church together and read the Bible like we used to.

When I turn around to go in and catch my bus home, my bag is gone. Shit! *Shit! My ticket!* I run into the terminal and look around, panicking. Did someone just take it by mistake? Surely no one thought there was anything valuable in my beat-up old bag—unless they watched me stuff my ticket inside. I run into the bathroom, and *holy crap*, there's my bag. Everything's dumped out—my clothes, all of it—spread all over the floor. This young girl comes out of a stall, and she's got tears and mascara running in dark smears down her bruised cheeks. Blood is crusted around her broken nose; it's smeared across her swollen face. I reach up to my own face, remembering the sting of my boyfriend's backhand.

She is holding her stomach with one hand, all bent over when she walks out. *I know the feeling, girlie,* I think. *Men are pigs.* She stops, staring at me through her one eye that isn't swollen shut. She's got this real scared look. That's when I realize she's wearing a pair of *my* pants and shirt, and clutching *my ticket* in her hand. I wanna push her against the wall and yank my ticket out of her grimy hand.

I wanna scream at her, "How could you steal from me! I have nothing!" I wanna hate her, hit her—*not* wanna help her. But instead I hear myself say to her, "Good luck," and I hold the bathroom door open for her to walk out.

She winces as she sidles past me, expecting a blow. When one doesn't come, she turns back and whispers, "Look in the bottom of the barrel."

I look at her like she's nuts, and just assume that she is, as I say kinda sarcastically to myself, "Yeah, I been scraping it, babe."

Helplessly I watch her board my bus, hear it close its big glass doors with a loud squeak, and suddenly feel very sick to my stomach as it pulls away. She presses her face to the window as she passes and mouths the words, "Thank you," through the glass.

There's nothing left to do now but go back to the bathroom and gather up my clothes. She'd stuffed my sweater into a large trash can in the corner. When I reach in to pull it out, I see what she meant by her strange parting words. In the bottom of the can, I find a nice size bag of cocaine. *This must be worth hundreds of dollars, maybe thousands.* I stuff it in my bag real quick and look around, suddenly paranoid that everyone in the bus terminal's watching me, knows what's in my bag, and is coming after it.

I walk north for a long ways before the anger erupts like a volcano. My parents' crap, my shitty childhood, my worthless boyfriends, my backstabbing friends... I start cursing up a steady stream toward everyone who's ever hurt me, disappointed me, humiliated me, or left me hanging. I snort some coke. *Screw all you assholes.* I keep walking, faster now, north. I start counting every disappointment I ever had or ever been, screaming them into the Florida night sky as I leave the city lights all behind me. I snort more coke. I decide then and there that I'm angry enough to walk all the way to Minnesota, February or not. I don't give a rat's ass. I let my hunger, my loneliness, and all that's ever been empty bubble up to the surface from the depths of my soul and exhale them out of my mouth in breathy plumes of vapor as I give voice to them in the cooling night. I snort more coke.

Tears come, and I let 'em. Hot and salty, down my cheeks, off my chin and onto the ground. I look around and see I've made it far out of the city. Beyond its lights, the stars shine dazzling and bright. I forgot how beautiful they are. I find myself alone in a field, spinning and watching the stars turn like a kaleidoscope through my tears. Dizzy, I fall to my knees in the mud. I grip my sweater with my hands in the chilly winter air to keep my fingers warm against my belly.

I feel this knot deep in my stomach again, a hard little golf ball in my gut. My heart is racing, beating too fast. I wish I hadn't been spinning around the field like an idiotic top, but even after I kneel real still in the mud, I feel like my brains are still rolling around in my head. My heart keeps going faster and faster and the golfball is growing bigger, like all of the tightly wound rubber bands inside are trying to burst right out of the shell. They want to push out of my belly like worms from a rotting carcass and spill everything I've been holding inside onto the mud. My blood is thumping in my ears so loud that I can't even hear myself when I scream, "God!"

I hear Him. "Daughter." My mind is flooding with the word, the voice, the presence, and suddenly I feel warmth throughout my entire body like radiant heat. I feel frozen. No, stuck. No, held fast! Held fast as I smile at the tenderness of His voice.

"Um, God?" I ask. I know immediately who is speaking to me.

"I will never leave you or forsake you."

"I know," and I did.

"You've forgotten something, haven't you, dear one? You've forgotten that you are mine. Do yout remember what you were taught long ago, sweet girl? The Lord is your shepherd. You lack nothing..."

I speak it with Him, remembering now. "He makes me lie down in green pastures, He leads me beside quiet waters, He refreshes my soul." Suddenly I see myself in a fragrant, flower- filled meadow, warm sun streaming down on my skin, white billowy clouds taking forms, reshaping themselves into a million moving pictures before my delighted eyes.

"Is this heaven?" I dreamily ask.

"This is my presence, daughter." He smiles and prompts me on: "He guides me along the right paths..."

I interrupt. "I missed those, Father. I took the wrong paths. So why are you here with me now?"

"Because you chose the most important path, my beautiful, prodigal daughter. You chose to believe in and love my son, Jesus. I read them, Daughter—the words of faith you wrote in your Bible long ago. I read them deeper still, etched upon your heart even when you'd forgotten who you are. You are my beloved daughter. Nothing can separate my love from you. Neither your choices nor the choices of others—in fact, nothing that this world throws at you can keep me from showing you my love over and over and over because it is who I am. I am love."

All of a sudden, I have a million flashbacks all at once. I remember Grandma's voice telling me about Jesus. I remember Bible verses and people being kind to me. I remember standing out under the stars, thinking about how amazing all the stuff was that Jesus did. I remember close calls when it had to have been God that got me out of all the rusty cages I got into, because nothing else could have done it.

Then God asks me, "Do you remember what comes next in David's song? Even though I walk through the darkest valley…"

"The bottom of the barrel," I joke.

"Yes, even though I walk through the bottom of the barrel, I will fear no evil," He laughs gently and waits for me to finish.

It all comes back to me, like when I was a kid up in front of the church next to my sister, saying it together, "For you are with me. Your rod and your staff, they comfort me. You prepare a table before me in the presence of my enemies. You anoint my head with oil; my cup overflows. Surely your goodness and love will follow me all the days of my life, and I will dwell in the house of the Lord forever. Will I?"

"Yes, you will. Forever." I can hear the smile in his voice, "But that wasn't your only question, was it, my beloved?"

"No, it's not. How has your goodness and love followed me all the days of my life? Because there've been plenty of times I didn't feel you. And never like I do tonight."

"Do you remember the story my Son told about the prodigal son? He ran away with his father's inheritance, wasted it away and was starving far away from home when he remembered."

"Remembered what?" I ask.

"He remembered who he was: a son of a merciful father. When he returned, his father saw him from a long way off and ran toward him, taking him into his arms and presence joyfully. That father is just one facet, one tiny piece of who I am. I'm also the father who walks with the prodigal along their journey. No matter how far off the goodness and love track they may wander, I keep putting stumbling blocks in their way. I protect them from some worse pain that way, or I allow some other pain, because pain is the only thing that seems to make my stubborn creation turn in a different direction. I remind the prodigal constantly of who they are. I whisper destiny, and gift them with creativity. I awe them with nature, move my followers into their paths, and fill their dreams with visions when their waking eyes are too clouded or busy or numb to see. And when the prodigal turns around I'm never a long way off. I'm right there, arms open wide to receive her, to hug and hold her forever."

"Like I saw in my dream!"

"Yes!" he giggles. "Have I answered your question?"

I think about it for a minute—the poor choices I've made, the ones I thought had pushed me out of His reach. More flashbacks come, but these flashes are different. I'm watching the things that happened, like scenes from a movie, but now it's like a lightning storm following me, from when I was born, right up to this moment. These flashes of bright light strike into the darkness, over and over again, changing the atmosphere around me.

I see myself as a little girl hiding under my bed, eyes closed, trying to make myself as invisible as I feel. Zap! Light hits me and when I open my eyes, my sister is sliding under there with me and I don't feel so alone. I see a real dark motel room where I'm so painfully sad that I just want my body to feel as dead as my heart does. Zap! Light hits me, and when my eyes adjust, there's a silver matchbook sitting in my hand.

Now it hits me—the reality is that He was always with me, just as He'd promised to be. I am so happy about seeing how He showed up over and over in my past, yet I know I need Him now more than ever before.

"Father, I'm sick. I did too much, didn't I?"

"Yes."

"I'm so tired, Father. Can I come home? Can I please just come home now?"

"Of course you can, my love. I'm right here. See me?"

And I do. He's standing in front of an ornate white bench in the expansive cloud meadow and opens His arms wide, grinning. I run to Him now, away from the dark valley, along the quiet waters and across the green pastures, a million steps all melded into one floating, flying sensation. I feel Him pull me up, up out of my broken, sick body, and then I'm in His arms, folded into His strength and love and joy. And here He gives me peace.

PART THREE:

My Sister's Keeper

Chapter Ten

JANE DOE

THE GRAVEL TRUCK MOVED SLOWLY, piled high with a load for a project in the city. The driver had driven it into the pits early, barely after sunrise. He had a number of orders to fill today and knew from experience he'd be slowed down by heavy traffic on the roads in and out of Daytona Beach. He'd taken care to tarp down the load tight so that gravel didn't fall off behind him. He'd nearly been jumped last year by a gang of bikers who'd insisted their cracked windshield was his fault. He wisely agreed to whatever they said and drove off.

The early morning fog he'd driven through was lifting as the sun's rays pushed through. Harvest was long past, and the fields were wet with the showers they'd had the past couple of dreary, cloudy days. Sitting high in the cab of his dump truck, he looked across the field, hoping to spot deer or foxes, as he did on so many mornings. The sun glinted off of something in the field, just off to the side. He peered closely as he drove slowly past, but slammed on his brakes when his mind registered what he saw.

He pulled over, shut off the truck and ran around the back toward the field. His heart racing, he heard himself

repeating breathlessly, "Oh God! Oh no! Oh God, no!"
He took a deep breath to calm himself and walked slowly
toward the bundle of clothes in the dirt. What he inhaled
told him what his brain refused to comprehend. It was a
body. He wretched his breakfast into the ditch, covered his
nose and mouth with one hand, and forced himself to step
closer. Black sweater, leopard patterned pants, black knee-
high boots, and the source of the glinting sunlight—blonde
hair.

She was face down in the mud, her hands in front of
her. He ran to his truck and got on his CB radio to reach
anyone who would listen. "There's a dead girl on the side
of the road. Somebody call the police!"

He was too shaken up to remember where he was until
his dispatcher repeatedly asked, "What's your twenty?" He
kept picturing his own teenage daughter at home, brown
haired and built round like her mother, getting ready for
school. He just wanted to get home to her now, make sure
she was okay, hold her tight and maybe never let her go
again.

He waited in the truck until the police came. A tall,
burly officer interviewed him while another walked over
to the body to take pictures. He was free to go, but stood
dumbly by the side of his truck watching the crime scene
investigators do their jobs. The tall officer joined his
buddy. "Looks like a prostitute to me." They rolled her
over to snap more pictures. The truck driver gasped. He
hadn't realized he'd walked closer to the body. There were
bugs, and a horrible smell wafted over the three men, who
involuntarily covered their mouths and stepped back.

The tall officer walked the driver to his truck, "We'll put some posters up around the bars and motels, and see if anybody knows who she is. There's no ID, nothing showing who she was or where she's from, except for all these tattoos, I guess. Hopefully somebody will know something about how Jane Doe ended up out here. Go home to your family, sir. I'm sorry you started your day out like this. And that she ended hers like this." The officer patted the truck driver on the back and frowned before turning to go to his squad car to call the morgue.

Nobody came forward who knew who she was. All the investigators knew was that she had a very high level of cocaine in her system when her body succumbed to the cold night air. And that she had good teeth. When she'd been at the coroner's office almost a week, a memo was sent to the public cemetery to complete the burial of her remains in an unmarked public gravesite.

There was no known family to contact. There were no missing person reports open on her. A DNA sample was taken and filed along with her clothing and two woven string bracelets. Her body, now torn apart by an investigative scalpel and probe, was put into a cheap pine box, lowered unceremoniously into a shallow hole and covered with dirt. Florida had swallowed her up in every conceivable way.

***

For the next thirteen years my family and I hoped for the best, refused to consider the worst, and made unsuccessful attempts to find her. Police in Iowa that next summer told me that I couldn't file a missing person's report because my sister would have been over the age of eighteen and "legally able to fall off the face of the earth if she wants to." This was misinformation, but what did I know? So I did numerous internet searches and lots of praying. I expected her to show up anytime, with her cocky grin and a wild story about what she'd been doing. I scoured prison records, newspapers and obituaries. I got in touch with the woman she'd stayed with, who told me she thought my sister had joined the circus.

I wanted to believe that she was alive, just really mad at us, or had amnesia, or even that she was in a mental hospital somewhere. Anything seemed better than considering the idea that I may never see her again.

Friends from our childhood and church asked about her and reassured me that they were praying for her and for us to find her. Life went on. I married and had six children, and my second daughter is a spitting image of her in looks and personality. I missed her every day but most torturously on her birthday and other family holidays when she should have been there to celebrate with us instead of becoming a fading memory.

Our family finally found an investigator who told us he could help, and over the next year, we began hoping again that she would be found. I daydreamed about hugging her tight as her information was put into the DOE Network website where volunteers scoured thousands of Florida missing persons, looking for a match with her tattoos and physical description. I relished the idea of telling her off as I submitted a DNA sample for them to put into their database. I wondered how I'd handle all the naughty things she'd probably teach my children as I saw the e-mails unfold. One of them said that her ID had been used to try to rent an apartment in 1997, four years after her disappearance. That was a great sign! We'd get her full story, mend whatever needed mending and be together again, the way it was supposed to be!

A few months later I sat down heavily as the voice on the other end of the phone spoke, "We've found her." I wanted the rest of it to go something like this, "She's alive and well, has a family of her own and wants to see you!" But it didn't.

That was the day I heard that my sister had overdosed on cocaine and died of hypothermia, alone on a remote road an hour and a half north of Daytona Beach in February of 1994. My street-smart, tough-as-nails little sister had lasted all of six months as a runaway. In spite of myself, I thought about the irony of a Minnesota girl going to Florida and freezing to death. But all I could feel was bone-deep, breathtaking pain. I curled into a fetal position on the floor and wailed her name. My children, concerned and confused, gathered around me and hugged me as I grieved. "Help Mommy's heart feel better," they prayed as I'd taught them. "Jesus, be close to Mommy," they prayed when I couldn't.

Chapter Eleven

KNOCKING ON HEAVEN'S DOOR

I HAVE BEEN FOLLOWING AFTER Jesus full time since I was eighteen years old, and He's surprised me plenty of times. My faith isn't a "check the box, I made it to church another Sunday, did my good deed for the day, wore a preachy t-shirt, blasted preachy music, prayed a preachy prayer, or, well, preached to someone" kind of faith. I'm not saying it's never been any of that, but as of right now, it's not even close. That's because He's walked through some heavy shit with me, intimately, and on the other side of grief has been abundance and freedom. I soak it up; it's water in a parched land. I grasp at it; it's life in a dying hand.

I gotta hear Him, see Him, feel Him. I have to collaborate with Him, know He's real, involved, and *for* me. I'm not talking about signs and wonders—although I've seen plenty of those, too. I'm talking about His presence. The best times for me to sense Him are when I'm quiet and alone with Him, or in an atmosphere of worship and prayer with Him. Sometimes, when I'm listening, He speaks. Sometimes, when I'm searching, He shows up. Sometimes, when I'm feeling small, He holds me, comforting and giving me courage to face my giants.

Even the smallest touch by this big God brings pervasive peace, joy and love, and I'm always craving more.

When I learned the circumstances of my little sister's death, I couldn't stand the thought of her walking alone along a dark highway, off the shoulder, through a muddy ditch and into a forlorn field. To think of her being so far from home and from anyone who loved her, dying alone, broke my heart. I cried into my pillow, "She was all alone."

I heard a strong, sure voice in my spirit correct me, "She was never alone. I was always with her, every step of the way." Knowing this was true brought me great comfort.

Years later, during a time of worship at church, I closed my eyes and a beautiful vision unfolded. In it, I walked into a great expanse I recognized immediately as heaven. On the other side of an open plaza sat an ornately decorated, white wrought iron park bench. God sat there, smiling and waving me over to come and sit with Him. I was flooded with joy at the thought of Him folding His arms around me and holding me close, and began to run toward Him. My daughter tugged on my hand, and I opened my eyes to reorient myself to my surroundings, but the vision still danced in my periphery, and I wrote it down quickly on the back of a bulletin.

A couple weeks later, I got up the nerve to ask the Lord, for the first time, where my sister was. I had never asked before because I had made assumptions based on her lifestyle choices, and because I'd never known her to make a decision to follow after Christ the way I had. It had been a definite line drawn in the sand for me, and I'd left a lot of darkness behind when I stepped toward the Light. As far as I'd seen, if she'd ever drawn a line, it was to remain stubbornly on the dark side of it.

But in this moment, I knew that no matter what the truth was, it was the right time for me to ask, and I could trust Him in the answering. So I closed my eyes and asked, "Lord, where is my little sister?"

Immediately I was transported back to the expanse of heaven I'd seen before. Across the plaza sat the white bench and the Lord was on it. Beside Him was my sister. He had His arm around her and they were both beaming and waving me over excitedly to join them. Her face was a picture of peace and joy.

When I opened my eyes, it was with tears of relief and gratitude. Without a shadow of a doubt, I now knew my sister was in heaven with the Lord, and I would definitely see her again.

God's redemption in our family didn't stop with His rescue of my life from the cycle of addiction and dysfunction, or of my sister from her broken, addicted body. It went on to rescue my mom from addiction and give her grace and strength to fight cancer and have a relationship with her children and grandchildren. He showed her how to have a relationship with Him and gave her the gift of remarriage to a godly, adoring husband. It went on to rescue my dad from addiction and show him a path to recovery and salvation through Jesus Christ, who, as it turns out, loves bikers and addicts, too.

God continues to reveal to me how tenderly He has my heart, and how mighty He is to save. I've revisited the farmhouse many times—emotionally, spiritually, and physically. I asked Him the hardest question a little girl can ask her Father. "Where were you? If you are all-knowing, all-present and all-powerful, just what were you doing when that man was in my bedroom? Watching?" I asked angrily, accusingly. I got no answer that day.

A week later, I was taking my daughter to a skin doctor appointment. We were sitting in the waiting room when security guards rushed in, threw open the doors on both sides of the room and wheeled a gurney past us. On it was a tiny baby, maybe a week old, in cardiac arrest. A nurse frantically did compressions on his little chest while his mother wailed and his father looked on, eyes wide with terror. Apparently the waiting room was the quickest way to the emergency room from the door the young couple had entered, carrying their obviously distressed newborn.

Feeling helpless, I began praying for the infant, the family, and the medical staff. As I trusted the baby to the Lord's hands, I saw it clearly in my mind's eye. As the nurse used two fingers to push the baby's chest, I saw the Lord's hand around his heart, protecting it, strengthening it, touching it—He was present. And I knew two things that day—the Lord would never let go of that baby's heart, and He had never let go of mine. Even in the midst of my childhood trauma, He was holding my heart, keeping it safe and strong and whole. He kept me unbroken.

Not long ago, I was driving in southern Minnesota and accidentally took a road I hadn't been on since I took it with my little sister almost twenty years before. I recognized a little white church on a corner and thanked God for the people who'd given me hope and safety within. Then I kept driving, slower now, toward the old farmhouse, missing my little sister and wondering at how different I felt this time. I was unafraid, as if the farmhouse and its ghosts had no power over me anymore. As I went past the driveway that used to lead to the house that had haunted my childhood and most of my adult life, I stopped in shock. It was gone! In its place stood a pretty, clean, new house. I laughed and shouted, "It's gone! Little sis, the damned thing's GONE!" I imagined either her or Jesus at the controls of the bulldozer, pushing away the rubble in the physical world the way God was pushing away my junk spiritually. And we laughed long and hard together — my sister's Keeper, my sister, and I.

EPILOGUE

When I woke up I wasn't in my own bed. I had gone to sleep in it such a short time ago that the memory lingered on the periphery of my mind. All of my children, their children and even some sleepy new great-grandchildren jammed into my bedroom, surrounding my bed and keeping vigil, if you could call it that. It was actually more like a party, which is what my husband and I had told them all for years that it should be. Passing into the next life was cause for celebration, we told them. Sure, we'd be missed and there was a time for grief, but our reunions on the other side would be that much sweeter because we had loved and been loved deeply.

One of the last things I heard before I slipped into slumber was my children singing my favorite song, by request; "He is a chariot, He fights for the lost. He is a chariot, the only rebel with a cause. People call upon His name, He reaches through the dark to save." The younger kids always laughed when their ancient little granny belted out the words to the old song. I had been too weak to sing or even speak for the last few days, so they sang for me.

The last thing I felt before my eyelids grew too heavy to lift open again was the sweet whiskery face of my husband, leaning over shakily to kiss my lips gently. He whispered in a gravelly voice, "I love you, honey." I felt him hold my hand, caressing it with his rough, calloused thumb. I smiled.

Here I was, running my final marathon, with my entire family there to cheer me on to the finish line. I was tired—

had been for a very long time. But I could see it now, and I reached for it the only way I knew how. I let go of the roomful of loved ones and let myself rest. I felt like I melted right into the mattress, so deep was my sleep.

I was awakened by colors. I smelled, heard, and felt them before I opened my eyes to see. My eyes saw smells, my nose felt sensations, and my ears tasted the sweet fragrances of incense dancing before my fingers. I should have been reeling with my topsy-turvy senses, but instead I stood there, taking it in, grinning wildly. I looked down at my feet to confirm that, yes, I was indeed standing. I hadn't done that in months.

Then I was twirling! Round and round, my arms outstretched, my head thrown back in laughter, my legs moving faster and faster as I spun, light and carefree. I ran and leaped and even did a cartwheel, something I'd never been able to do before. And when the reality of where I was fully set in, I immediately looked around for *Him*.

He was nearby, sitting on an ornate white bench, smiling and waving me over to come sit with Him. It was a familiar scene, but something was missing. He was alone on the bench. He saw my question and spoke, "Come, my glorious daughter. You have waited such a long time for this day. You have done well, my child and I love you!" He stood to walk toward me and I ran into His arms and let Him fold me in. I forgot all else in that moment with Him.

He said, "In my house there are many rooms. Would you like to see yours, daughter?" I walked excitedly, hand in hand with Him to the place He'd prepared just for me.

There was a beautiful bed and a shelf filled with decorative boxes. Curious, I walked to them and looked to Him for permission to open one. "What are these, Father?"

"They are your treasures, dear. You may do what you like with them. I have been saving them for you throughout your whole life." He watched, smiling, as I pulled down an ivory-covered box with little roses, my favorite flowers, carved delicately into the lid.

I carefully opened it and more colors danced out, swirling around my head. Suddenly I remembered them—all the cute things my children had said, all the special moments I'd been too busy to write about in a journal, all the mental snapshots I'd taken, wistfully desiring above all else to hold the feelings in my heart as distinctly as a photograph holds an image for the eyes. "Thank you!" I whispered.

"You are welcome. There's so much more, daughter. It will take an eternity for you to even begin to unpack all of the wonderful gifts I have for you. You began that eternity as a girl, and I have loved your eagerness to find my treasures. I will show you how you entertained angels, many times, unaware, even my own Son. I will show you all of my interventions, though you have been astute in readily seeing many of them and giving me glory. You will enjoy seeing so much more with the new eyes I have given you in this new body."

"Thank you, Father."

"You will continue to live a life of adventure and abundance, but here, in the fullness of my presence and love, nothing can harm you. Nothing can hinder you. You are free indeed, my sweet daughter, forever and ever."

I knelt at His feet then, in worship and gratitude. "Holy, Holy, Holy is the Lord God Almighty..." I joined the chant of the angels surrounding His throne. (Somehow He was on His throne at the same time He was in my room with me.) I heard another voice beside me at His feet, "Holy, Holy, Holy is the Lord God Almighty..." I recognized it immediately. It was *her*!

The Father laughed as I barrel-rolled my sister in a hug. "I knew you were here! I knew it! I missed you so much!" I couldn't let go of her. We sat on the end of my bed and talked for hours, maybe. Time really isn't measured when you're sitting there somewhere on a continuum of eternity.

Suddenly I remembered what I'd waited so long to tell her and blurted out, "Hey, it's gone! Somebody bulldozed the farmhouse to the ground!"

She laughed. "I know. It was my idea, like in Forrest Gump when he knocks down Jenny's house. Father and I love that movie!"

"You watch movies here?"

"Well, yeah, but only good ones."

"You mean like, PG or G?"

"No, I mean like good quality, you know—good storyline, good acting, redemption, the ones that show the Father's heart. You can let go of all that religious stuff here, you know. Anything creative comes from God. It just gets twisted a bit sometimes in the expression." She spread her arms wide and grinned, "It's so fun here, you know! It's a place of ridiculous joy!"

"I really don't know exactly what that means yet, but I

saw it on your face when I saw the vision of you with God all those years ago."

She looked deep into my eyes and said earnestly, "That was so kind of Him to show you that. He knew you were really worried about me. That was a really long time ago, in human years." She grinned suddenly and went on, "Which leads me to the question I've been waiting, what, like, seventy years to ask you."

"Yes, what's that?" I smiled at her teasing tone.

"What took you so long to get here, Nance?"

"Heather, I wasn't racing."

AUTHOR'S NOTE

Dear Reader,

Well, now you know that the girls are real. I am the big sister. Heather is my little sister. This is her memorial, my attempt to give her a voice and find healing through using my own. But it is so much more.

This is the first book I started after I sensed the Lord telling me to pick up the pen a while back. I wrote the first couple chapters, then set it aside as a new story unfolded for me to write. It was a fiction novel called NUBBY. It was so fresh in my waking mind that I couldn't *not* write it. After I successfully published and shared my first *baby* with the world, I asked the Lord, *What next?* I became obsessed with reading all that I could about sex trafficking, especially in the U.S. but I wasn't sure why until one day when I was riding my Harley. I was alone on my annual pilgrimage over Heather's birthday when I heard in my spirit one simple sentence. "Heather was trafficked."

Suddenly I knew what my next book must be. It had to be her story. As I sat down to write it, however, I realized immediately that her story and mine were entwined, and I could tell hers best by sharing ours.

I pulled out my previous writing and sat dumbly, numbly avoiding even thinking about where to begin. Being well enough acquainted with grief, I knew this journey would take me to places I'd long avoided. But being well enough acquainted with the God who was calling me to the task,

I knew that He could be trusted to take me through this journey of healing.

I took my bike out to a park and sat by a tree, completely at a loss for how to start. The download that came gave me all I needed to continue. In my mind, I saw every step outlined—title, main parts, chapters and chapter titles. I even knew that I wanted to try to use different voices in first person for the two sisters, though I had no idea how. I typed them feverishly into my phone and decided to trust God with each successive step.

Walking through darkness with my little sister was one of the hardest things I've ever done. Presenting the book to my parents was even worse. I decided early on that I would not share this book with anyone without the blessing of my mom and dad. I sat there with the finished first draft, praying that my intentions would show through. It was never my intent to make my parents villains, but just to show addiction as the real enemy of our childhood. I focused on the darkest times in our lives and wrote them as if they were the norm. They both understand why and have expressed their views in healthy ways, and I think have forgiven me. Then they courageously told me to publish it; it would help others. I can't even tell you how proud I am of them for that!

My parents were kids trapped in their own areas of bondage when we were born. Neither of them were equipped for marriage or family, yet I am forever grateful that they chose to let me live despite other options available to them at the time. What they have given me as their daughter—wit, creativity, strength, humility and ridiculously youthful good looks—makes me thankful that I am theirs. Even through their dysfunctional actions and irresponsible decisions, I knew they loved me and were proud of me. That foundation ran deep and gave me power to be resilient and to receive love from others as I grew up and my sphere of influence increased.

It's important that I say right now that this book is about fifty percent memoir and fifty percent realistic fiction, and nobody really needs to know which is which. I took creative story-telling license with details in this book, but the heart of the story is one-hundred percent accurate. All the events could have happened just as I described, but in all honesty, I'm not sure that they did. Memory fails, perspectives change over time, some gaps have been filled by the Holy Spirit, and many more remained empty. I wrote much of Heather's part as I envisioned in my heart and mind, only to have events and descriptions confirmed by the police reports I later received. Until I get to heaven I don't expect to know exactly what happened to my beautiful sister, but I doubt it will matter then.

So, what were my intentions with this book? First of all, I needed to be faithful with taking the steps the Father put in front of me, no matter how difficult they were. His intentions were to show me His faithfulness. I wanted to be careful not to show the power of darkness, but rather the inevitability of darkness and the persistence and provision of the Father. His intention was to show me over and over again that all people are within His grasp, no matter how their lives may look to the casual or judgmental observer. I intended to encourage people, the Church especially, not to grow weary in doing good, for even the smallest things done with great love mean something—sometimes everything—to someone. He intended to remind me of the same.

Now that you have heard our voices, I hope you will trust the Keeper as you use your own.

A beloved daughter,
and sister,
Nancy

U.S. Sex Trafficking

Human trafficking exists all over the United States

- The average entry age of American minors into the sex trade is 12-14 years old.

- Many victims are runaway girls who have already suffered sexual abuse as children.

- Foreign nationals are also brought into the U.S. as slaves for labor or commercial sex through force or fraud.

- The prevalence and anonymity of the internet has fueled the rapid growth of sex trafficking, making the trade of women and children easier than ever before.

Sex trafficking occurs when people are forced or coerced into the commercial sex trade against their will. Child sex trafficking includes any child involved in commercial sex. Sex traffickers frequently target vulnerable people with histories of abuse and then use violence, threats, lies, false promises, debt bondage, or other forms of control and manipulation to keep victims involved in the sex industry. Sex trafficking exists within the broader commercial sex trade, often at much larger rates than most people realize or understand. Sex trafficking has been found in a wide variety of venues of the overall sex industry, including residential brothels, hostess clubs, online escort services, fake massage businesses, strip clubs, and street prostitution.

National Human Trafficking Resource Center

The National Human Trafficking Resource Center (NHTRC) is a national, toll-free hotline, available to answer calls and texts from anywhere in the country, 24 hours a day, 7 days a week, every day of the year.

The NHTRC is a program of Polaris Project, a non-profit, non-governmental organization working exclusively on the issue of human trafficking. It is not a government entity, law enforcement or an immigration authority.

Call **1-888-373-7888** or text HELP or INFO to BeFree (233733):

- To report a tip,
- To connect with anti-trafficking services in your area, or
- To request training and technical assistance, general information or specific anti-trafficking resources.

What regular folks are saying about *NUBBY,*
An unthinkable crime. An unlikely redemption.

5.0 out of 5 stars **Awesome!** July 15, 2013
By **JillyBeans**
The story pulled me in immediately... it had new material from what I normally read (I read all genre of books). It identifies real life situations happening in our country and around the world today. A must read for those wanting to make a difference in the world. I can't wait to read the sequel or anything else this writer produces. Timely, well-written, graphic with the feeling that I am there experiencing it myself. Thank you, Nancy!

5.0 out of 5 stars **Worth the risk! READ IT!**
What a wonderful debut novel! I would have never guessed if someone didn't tell me. WOW! This is a must read! From page one, I was hooked. The story line and plot were original and exciting. I fell in love with the characters, even the evil ones! That is saying something...I cannot wait to see what comes next!

5.0 out of 5 stars **READ NUBBY!**
Nubby is refreshingly honest and culturally relevant to the times in which we currently live. Every chapter hooked me with suspense like an episode of 24 — I couldn't put it down! Nancy Paul touches on many issues facing the world and the Church — human trafficking, homelessness, despair, the reality of wounded souls wounding others, human greed,

and last but definitely not least, passive and detached Christians who do not get involved. What is refreshing is the truth portrayed in the Power and Movement of a Holy and Loving God, how He is intricately involved in the lives of His children and leading those who love Him into grace and salvation. I was moved to tears and to praising the Lord out loud as He made a way where there seemed to be no way for the characters in this story. This fictional novel will confront your real life in how you view your place in this world, how you view the place of the Church in this world, and how you view the Father's place in your circumstances. There is Hope in even the darkest night! I highly recommend this book.

5.0 out of 5 stars **Nubby is supernaturally magic**
This story is so satisfying on so many different levels. It has an almost supernatural magic to the way the pieces of the story fit together. I love the characters—even the evil ones—because every part of humanity is exposed and in the end redemption feels so dang right. So good it gave me chills.

5.0 out of 5 stars **Love this book!**

5.0 out of 5 stars **Riveting!**

4.0 out of 5 stars **Solid characters, interesting twists**

5.0 out of 5 stars **Really Great Book. Captures your attention and won't let it go.**

5.0 out of 5 stars **Can't put it down!**

5.0 out of 5 stars **Fantastic book**

5.0 out of 5 stars **GREAT story! Couldn't put the book down!!**

5.0 out of 5 stars **EXCELLENT!!! This is a must read!!!**

5.0 out of 5 stars **Fabulously written**

5.0 out of 5 stars **Excellent read!**

5.0 out of 5 stars **Wonderful!**

5.0 out of 5 stars **Amazing debut!!**

5.0 out of 5 stars **Thought provoking**

5.0 out of 5 stars **Truly inspired voice**

5.0 out of 5 stars **Wonderful book! It draws you in and doesn't let you go until the end!**

5.0 out of 5 stars **Fascinating and thrilling adventure**

5.0 out of 5 stars **Amazingly AMAZING!**

Made in the USA
San Bernardino, CA
06 August 2017